MW00380671

The Week
from
Heaven
and
Hell

by
Duke Southard

A Tribute
To Our Son
Captain Gary Scott Southard
United States Army
June 26, 1962- May 14, 1992

The Week from Heaven and Hell

Copyright © 2010 Duke Southard. All rights reserved. No part of this book may be reproduced or retransmitted in any form or by any means without the written permission of the publisher.

Published by Wheatmark®
610 East Delano Street, Suite 104
Tucson, Arizona 85705 U.S.A.
www.wheatmark.com

International Standard Book Number: 978-1-60494-382-5
Library of Congress Control Number: 2009940288

Dedication

This book is dedicated to my family whom I love with all my heart:

To Barbara, whose courage during and after the time described in this book was an inspiration to so many, especially me, and whose presence makes me count my blessings every day.

To Jeri and Pam, who probably are unaware of the strength I draw from them and how fortunate I feel to have such outstanding young women for daughters.

Acknowledgements

This tribute is written primarily from my perspective and my memory of events. However, I would thank our many friends and family members who so freely shared their thoughts when asked for them. As the book indicates, I can't imagine how we would have managed to endure without their support and willingness to do anything to help.

I would thank Jennifer Coulter, my objective reader, who was not in our lives at the time of Gary's death. Her insight and perceptive comments eliminated much of my tunnel vision approach to a subject so close to me. I appreciate her unselfish sharing of time and effort to help make this tribute what it is.

My grateful thanks to Ray Lord, copy editor extraordinaire, for his time-consuming efforts on this book and for still having the ability to make me laugh.

Finally, my very special thanks go to my former "prize" pupil, Linda Jones, who provided a fresh perception on this project, thereby improving it immensely.

About the author...

Duke Southard is a retired public high school English teacher and Library/Media Specialist. He has published professional articles in *Media and Methods Magazine* and served as president of the New Hampshire Educational Media Association. In 1997, he was presented with an "EDie," the New Hampshire Excellence in Education Award for his contribution to the school library/media profession in the state. His educational credentials include a BS from Villanova University, an MA in English Education from Glassboro State University and a CAGS in Library/Media Technology for Boston University.

He is married and the father of three children. He lived in Tuftonboro, New Hampshire for almost forty years before moving to Green Valley, Arizona.

He is the author of two novels. His first, *A Favor Returned*, was published in May, 2000 by Peter Randall and distributed by University Press of New England. His second, *Agent for Justice*, was published in October, 2003 by Hot House Press of Cohasset, Massachusetts. He also is the author of *The Nick: A Vision Realized*, published in May, 2007.

Visit the author's website at www.dukesouthard.com for information on his work and free programs for schools, libraries and community groups.

Table of Contents

Author's Note
(Not To Be Ignored!)

Weeks begin on Sundays and end on Saturdays. They are of a duration of seven days and we use them as convenient markers of time passed or yet to come. To simplify the title, I've chosen to use the term "week" but the actual time covered in the book is nine days. In my mind, a definitive beginning and a definitive end bracket the events depicted but their impact continues to be felt even now, sixteen years later. A nine-day week would be more useful to describe the heaven that began that time and the hell that ended it.

The story is told from three perspectives, each represented by a distinct style of font. When retelling factual events, I used a common style. With the realization that most people will not and could not know parts of the story that are "family-unique," I reserved a simple italicized font for flashbacks, anecdotes and other information pertinent to the narrative. These parts of the story will allow you personal glimpses into our lives as family, as friends, and as members of a community. Those who inhabit the circle in which this story takes place deserve to be personalized, to be made real and the details revealed in these sections accomplish this. Finally, the bold italicized print relates events for which I have no explanation and which, to most people, will likely represent only coincidences. I share these with the hope that you will simply consider them. Feel free to speculate, discuss, hypothesize and let your mind take it where it will. Mine already has and I see no reason to deny the same experience to you. Please take them in the spirit in which I share them.

As I was writing this, I told my family that my goal was to provide a fitting tribute to an exceptional young man who deserved to live out his life, a good person who had much to offer this somewhat warped world. With that goal in mind, I would implore you not to skip any of the sections for I believe in the concept that the sum is always made up of the parts. The tribute moves far beyond our beloved son, however, and the effect of the tribute would be diluted if any part of the story of our faith, our family, our friends and our community was not included. It is a devastatingly sad story and the tragedy that struck that beautiful May afternoon remains firmly fixed in the realm of disbelief.

I would pray that the story of the powers that brought us through it is uplifting in some way to each of you. It could never be a happy story but I believe that it can be a positive one.

Foreword

Most of my friends and members of my family would agree that I have any number of strange idiosyncrasies. However, even those closest to me would not have known about one that colors much of my thinking when crucial events occur in my life

I find that I have a tendency to frame these events in the context of the rest of the inhabitants on this bulging planet. I've always believed that during the vast variety of our human adventures, we could be assured that someone else in the world must be having a similar experience to ours, possibly even at the exact same time. Surely, among the billions of humans careening through the complex experience of existing in our world, one or more could identify precisely with what was happening to me. Now, I don't mean to indicate that I've never shared this concept with anyone. I have found, however, that when I do start to explain it, most people seem to begin backing away, psychologically if not physically, as though searching for some distraction to end the conversation.

As my wife and I joined our lovely young daughter-in-law to assist her in choosing a casket for our twenty-nine-year-old son, the theory flitted through my churning and chaotic mind. I speculated about the odds. Could there be another father somewhere who would walk his daughter down the matrimonial aisle less than eight hours after visiting a showroom full of those final vehicles designed to chauffeur their occupants into eternity?

The hushed voice of the funeral director drifted over the open lids of the well-padded, silk lined "repositories," just one of so many euphemisms used that day and the grief filled days following. The quiet scene might have been taking place in a Mercedes Benz showroom, where the clientele are shocked into an awed silence by both the automobiles and the attached price tags.

The emotional devastation of the situation we were facing clearly defined what I felt was an unspeakable, shattering reality. I couldn't imagine anyone across the thousands of square miles of the globe feeling what each of us felt as we followed the whispered instructions from the director to run a finger over the soft silk lining of an especially well designed casket.

"Quite reasonable for the quality," the compassionate director said.

The inanity of the remark attracted my attention. Nothing that he had said was anything but genuine and I felt guilty as I fought the urge to scream at him. My resistance was successful but we were, after all, not selecting parlor furniture here. Then, in a strangely ambivalent moment, I found myself smiling as the environment swam before me, becoming more surreal by the second. The mental anguish of losing such a vital and compassionate human being to a random quirk of misfiring electrical currents in a robust and healthy heart overwhelmed me. After all, he was a soldier, in peak condition. He had recently passed a required physical for learning to fly. The medical terminology seemed simple yet upon examination was impossibly obscure. Nothing could convince me that a twenty-nine year old should have died of a heart problem.

Less than forty-eight hours before, the week from Heaven, the prelude to our younger daughter's wedding, had tumbled through a descent into Hell in a matter of seconds. Once more, I grasped desperately for the knowledge that we were not alone, could not be alone.

I silently wondered how we would ever will ourselves through the wedding just hours away.

*   *   *

Chapter One
The Descent Into Hell
Thursday, May 14, 1992
My Worst Day

The alarm had a surreal quality about it that morning. I couldn't believe that the buzzing sound was anything but a figment of a hazy, nebulous dream. We had even gone completely out of character and allowed an extra fifteen minutes of sleep. It hadn't been difficult to convince Barbara to sleep along with the "kids" and take advantage of her vacation time. She simply fumbled for the clock, her practiced fingers deftly finding the alarm switch as instinct rolled me from my bed. I stumbled toward the closet. After several minutes of fumbling, I found everything I needed to get ready for school. After a quick shower, I crept down the steps to inhale an English muffin and coffee before the car pool arrived. I remember sitting there hunched over my coffee, thinking how much I appreciated the time spent with the family the night before. The discussion of our best and worst days inspired by Billy Crystal and the "City Slickers" film had been deep but still lighthearted. Our family was clearly blessed and our closeness never was more apparent than it was that night. Remnants of the conversation continued to surface in my mind as I sipped my coffee and thought about my last day at school before the event-filled weekend. My only regret was that one of our girls, daughter Jeri, was not able to be a part of the evening.

*   *   *

Jeri, carrying much of the baggage that the "middle child syndrome" implies, wrote from her heart:

"There are many images etched in my mind that I will never forget," Jeri begins her eloquent expression of some rather private thoughts.

"Even when I'm as old as Nan or even with a case of Alzheimer's Disease, the memories of that day will haunt me. In the years that have followed, I've been constantly amazed at how we stew in the memories surrounding a loved one's death. The facts of the death take on a life of their own and one must battle to put the life, not the death, in the foreground. With the minute-by-minute details still vivid in my mind, there's one fragment of time that is perhaps the most poignant. When Mom and Pam rushed to the hospital, leaving me with my two little boys and the emptiness of not knowing, I had the unwanted task of calling Dad at Kennett to tell him what little news we did have."

*   *   *

As I was finishing the abbreviated breakfast, I became aware of the door to Gary's old bedroom opening. I listened as Ollie come cascading down the stairs, his short and aged legs barely able to stay ahead of his body. Gary, muttering and probably swearing under his breath, followed close behind him. Ollie always seemed to sense when people were desperate to sleep late and he chose those times to awaken all those that he could, his frantic face-licking convincing them of an equally desperate need to go out. With an unintelligible grunt, Gary pushed by my chair and opened the door. Ollie, having accomplished his purpose, stood by the door, looking up at his true master as though about to change his mind. Gary supplied a slight but firm nudge with a bare foot and the issue whether the dog would stay in or go out was decided. He turned and looked at me, a bit of the haze of sleep clearing, and smiled. Not a word was spoken as he turned to go back to bed. I smiled at his back as he left the room. It was the last time I saw him alive.

I still reel with profound sadness on occasions when I think of that time with wonder. Why didn't I tell him how much I loved him?

* * *

We were tricked into accepting Ollie into the family and Gary played a major role in the clever scheme. Several months before Ollie became an integral part of our existence, I had taken a deaf and virtually blind sixteen-year-old Snoopy to our veterinarian for the last time.

"No more animals" became a familiar parental litany recited on a daily basis. One evening late in the fall of Gary's junior year in high school, I arrived home late from school to be greeted at the door by an adorable black ball of fur, its tiny tail a wagging blur. (Is there such a thing as an ugly puppy?) Gary and his sisters looked at me, seeing right through my initial "No way" reaction. I picked up the puppy, an unusual mixture of miniature collie and poodle with a few other breeds no doubt lurking in its genes as well. The three faces carried the look of children much younger, anticipation glowing in their eyes as if waiting to be called downstairs on Christmas morning. I assumed the typical father's posture.

"Wait until your mother gets home from choir and we'll see what she has to say." I announced, stepping aside from a decision until another scapegoat was available. Snoopy had indeed been our dog, not theirs, so technically their feeling that they had been denied the right of every child to have a puppy was correct. We all waited for Barbara, they with their agenda and I with mine..

The mudroom door hadn't closed behind her before the new arrival came to a skidding stop at her feet after a headlong dash from the living room. Gary was prepared.

"He's just visiting," he said, fending off Barbara's immediate negative reaction with his initial ploy. Then, he quickly launched into his well-rehearsed justification. First, he explained that this was the last of the litter and if someone didn't adopt it, and soon,

the owner would have to drown the poor thing. Now it happened that we knew the gentle owner quite well and the thought of him harming any living creature was out of the question. Gary then reached into his pocket and produced a most convincing document, a document obviously showing careful preparation. It was a promissory note, signed by all three children and duly notarized by a friend, coincidentally the brother of the pup's owner. The note promised that all three children would assume responsibility for all aspects of the puppy's care, even including a clause that swore a commitment to "lifetime care." It was so cleverly conceived that my potential scapegoat and I shared a shoulder shrug and a resigned affirmative nod. I remember later that night making a comment that there was absolutely no possibility that John Stockman could ever have drowned that puppy.

"I know that," Barbara answered. "We were trapped," she said with a smile.

The puppy was dubbed Olio by Gary's Latin teacher, the word meaning "all mixed up" in Latin. For the next fifteen years, Ollie was a fixture in the Southard household, long after the "kids" moved on with their lives. Of course, they conveniently forgot the promissory note in spite of my habit of resurrecting it at opportune times when they were home for visits. We always felt that he was their dog, tolerating us but reserving his most enthusiastic greetings for them whenever they returned home. His final trip to the vet came in November of 1992, the same year that we lost Gary.

*   *   *

The car pool that beautiful spring morning consisted of Diane and Gary Tepe, neighbors and colleagues who were rapidly becoming best friends, and me. Kennett High School lay twenty-eight miles to the north and on those days when I made the trip alone, the ride seemed interminable. Gary had joined the Kennett faculty as a guidance counselor midway through the school year while Diane and I had been colleagues and car pool partners for almost four years. Gary added his keen sense of humor to the already congenial pool and his sharing of the burden of driving supplied a welcome relief to the two of us who had survived many harrowing winter trips traveling north on the treacherous two-lane highway that was Route 16. The natural beauty of the White Mountains formed an inspirational backdrop for the drive and on those rare days when no one felt like talking, the mountain scenery silently spoke to all of us.

This morning ride became a one sided conversation, more like a monologue, as I bored my partners with a detailed description of the entire evening before. As the odd man out, I rode in the back seat and remember leaning into the space between the two front bucket seats, one arm resting on each of them, talking practically non-stop until we entered the parking lot. I described in detail the abortive attempt to play golf, the wonderful dinner and conversation at Chequers Villa and the double feature topped off by the remarkably candid discussion of best and worst days. The narrative easily filled the forty-minute journey. My partners likely were relieved to see the trip come to an end.

My request for a personal business day on Friday had been approved weeks before by an understanding principal requiring only a minimum of explanation. Surely, the expectations of a father of the bride demanded that I needed a full day off before the wedding. Unmentioned but I'm certain acknowledged by the golfing principal was the possibility that a pre-wedding golf outing with many of the early arriving guests would take up much of the time on Friday. Anticipating a long weekend filled with a full schedule of events surrounding the wedding, I knew that this workday would pass quickly.

The three of us parted after running the gauntlet through the crowded cafeteria. The students anxiously waited for the tone that allowed them to move out into the building for the intense daily socializing before the start of school. Diane, viewed as one of the most dedicated teachers in the school, promised to conclude her school duties as quickly as possible, well aware of how anxious I was to return home to the ever increasing activity around the house.

A small knot of teachers stood by the library door as I made my way up the steps and within a few minutes, I was paddling to stay afloat in what Diane often referred to as the "whitewater" of Kennett High School. Several of the teachers followed me in and without even taking off my jacket I began hauling out film projectors and VCR's, finding reference books and filling last minute requests for resources and supplies needed for the lessons of the day. When the 7:15 tone sounded, the room filled with students frantically searching for a quiet place to finish the previous night's assignment before homeroom began in fifteen minutes.

The day was no different than any other in the library, the excitement of dealing with such a variety of human beings and the wide diversity of their needs blurring the time. The most recalcitrant student couldn't have altered my cheerful mood that day; I would admit that as I went about the business of running the facility, my mind frequently wandered into pleasant daydreams of the long weekend ahead.

                              *   *   *

We had arranged with Paul and Sally Downing, the owners of Indian Mound Golf Course where we hold a membership, to keep a running tab for the week as Gary wanted to play every chance he could. On any number of occasions that morning, as I gazed through the huge library window at the magnificent sight of a snow covered Mt. Washington reflecting the early spring sun, I thought enviously of Gary and Barbara squeezing in nine holes that morning. As the day warmed quickly, we opened a few of the small casement windows and the uniquely fresh smell of spring wafted through the library. It was not difficult at all for me to vicariously experience the warmth of the sun on their faces as they stood on the first tee, staring down the verdant fairway. However, the Kennett Library, always a busy facility, allowed little opportunity for indulging in the delightful family golf outing fantasies. The constant student and staff requests for assistance eventually sent them scuttling out of my mind.

* * *

True to his West Point military training, Gary arranged his schedule for the day with precision. After his round of golf with his mom, he would take a long run into Canaan Valley. He loved dabbling in cooking and had reserved Thursday as the day he would prepare his special recipe for stuffed shells. His plan included putting the shells together before driving his grandmother, Nan, to her doctor's appointment in Laconia. It was sure to be yet another evening with the kind of family camaraderie where the siblings told childhood tales on each other. As the harmless secrets unfolded and the naïve parents groaned, the "children" would be relishing their positions as informers. I couldn't wait.

* * *

The day at home proceeded closely to the plan. The golf, the long country run, and the stuffed shells were all completed well within time to leave for Laconia. Although Nan, a healthy eighty-four year old, still had her driver's license, we all agreed that any driving she did should be restricted to the familiar short trips directly to Wolfeboro and back. Driving to Laconia certainly was out of the question and Gary's stature as favorite grandson and, the girls would argue, favorite grandchild, climbed yet another notch as he offered to drive her to the appointment.

* * *

Marion Ortlieb Gross, Doctor of Osteopathy, should be considered a pioneer. Her graduation from The Philadelphia College of Osteopathic Medicine in 1929 demonstrated strength of character and a determination that earned her the respect of all who knew her. When she moved to New Hampshire, she left a small practice behind and assumed a sort of matriarchal existence as "Nan," the consummate game player and companion for her three grandchil-

dren. Gary, as the oldest grandchild and more importantly, the only grandson, was arguably her favorite. When the invitation came for the fiftieth reunion of her class at PCOM, it was Gary who convinced her that she must attend, volunteering to be her escort. Unable to resist the encouragement of her grandson, a high school senior, she grudgingly agreed. The cliché about a picture being worth a thousand words is certainly true. The photo taken of the two of them at the reunion dinner tells the story. The tall handsome young man sits next to the graceful elderly woman, the pride shining in her eyes. Not only had they traveled over four hundred miles but they were the only grandmother/grandson couple in attendance.

*   *   *

As the library filled with students for the final period of the day, I remember thinking about how fast this day had passed. Generally, the higher the level of anticipation, the more slowly the clock ticks but Diane's Kennett "whitewater" theory cascaded through the library as well and the periods blurred together with student activity. Now, I faced the final forty-five minutes of the day and a quick cleanup of details and my long weekend would start.

Jean Green, a professional librarian, volunteered her invaluable expertise several days a week and sat cataloging books in my office. With several potentially difficult students in the library for the last period of the day, I decided that I would make my presence known a little more than usual. I worked at a table in the center of the library, well aware that any attempt at appearing stern was futile under the circumstances. Just as many of the students, I had one mental foot out of the door already.

Fifteen minutes into the period, I heard the telephone ring in my office and watched through the small window as Jean answered it, motioning that the call was for me. I glanced around at my students, all of whom were engaged or pretending to be engaged in the "productive activity" I required in the library. As I walked across the room toward the office, I thought about who the caller might be. A pleasant telemarketer from Salem Press often called at this time of day and when I reached the phone, I was sure that I would hear her familiar greeting. I lifted the receiver and said a cheery hello, fully expecting Palma's usual "Hi, Al!" Instead, I heard Jeri's voice, only detecting the slight trembling after her first sentence careened through the synapses several times before penetrating and settling into blunt understanding.

My beloved daughter, now forced into the impossible position of "liaison," rose to the occasion as she had in so many athletic competitions before. All of those, she had to admit, lost much significance in this crushing situation.

$$* \quad * \quad *$$

Jeri's description continued.

"I'll never forget the seemingly endless minutes it took for him to come to the phone. With no time to rehearse what I might say, only the knowledge of what my experience in life thus far had taught me, I blurted out the words that came into my mouth and waited for the welcome reassurance that is my dad. I will never forget that moment, for in that moment it all changed. For the first time in my life, I was the reassurer. I managed to utter the words 'It's all right, Dad, he'll be ok' before he broke the phone connection with a hurried "I'll be right home." His life had changed in an instant, just as ours had just moments before."

$$* \quad * \quad *$$

Time may indeed seem to stand still. An adrenaline rush such as one might experience during the stress of an automobile accident or some equally traumatic event can cause the world to go by in slow motion. There are times when the shock of what you are hearing is so surreal, so outrageous, that it imposes the same effect.

"Hi Dad," Jeri said. The quaver in her voice became just slightly stronger as I gripped the back of my chair. I knew that Jeri and our grandsons were scheduled to come to our house for the day and stay for dinner as the heaven of the week continued with another family gathering. I'm sure my instinctive conclusion was that I would be asked to run an errand or pick something up at the store. There could be no other reason for her to call me at school. Before I could respond, she continued.

"Nan and Gary have been in an accident."

I waited, looking through the window as some of the activity on the floor of the library was subtly changing from productive to less productive. Later, when I tried to tell Diane and Gary exactly what she said, I was amazed that only pieces of it remained in my memory. Obviously, I followed her account with intense interest. When she said that the woman who called to inform our household about the accident mentioned that Gary was being given CPR, I corrected her.

"You mean Nan," I told her with a desperate finality. I was wrong.

The conversation only lasted about three minutes, during which it became clear that I needed to get home right away. Pam and Barb had left right away to drive to the scene, over ten miles from our home. With Jeri's reassuring "He'll be ok" still echoing in my ear, I told her I'd be home as quickly s I could and put the receiver down. I stared out of my office window at two or three students who were now clearly disengaged from anything approaching productive activity. They needed to be reprimanded but their behavior, so important to me just moments before, no longer mattered.

Jean Green appeared at my office doorway, ready to resume her cataloging. I blurted out the gist of the phone call then pushed passed her and stumbled down the single flight of stairs to a lower hallway and soon stood at Diane's classroom door. She, as usual, was completely immersed in her class but finally caught my increasingly frantic waves. I turned and leaned against the wall as I saw her coming. In short, staccato sentences, I managed to give her the information she needed. Within minutes, she had the necessary coverage arranged for her class and left to go find Gary in the Guidance Office. By two o'clock, we were leaving the Kennett parking lot. Unlike the morning commute, I reclined in the back seat, my head leaning back and eyes staring at the headliner as if it contained some hidden answer for me. I realized at one point on the trip home that despite the warmth of the day, I was shivering. Most of the trip was silent, only an occasional "I can't believe this!" emanating from my position in the rear seat and reassurances that everything would be all right from the front. It was the longest twenty eight-mile trip I'd ever taken.

Jeri, our two young grandsons close behind, greeted the car as we turned in the driveway. I was out and hugging her in what seemed a single motion. She had heard nothing further from Barbara or Pam and assumed they had gone on to the hospital in Laconia. Diane and Gary refused to allow me to drive to the hospital alone and we immediately piled into their car once again for yet another forty minute journey, this time to Lakes Region General Hospital, leaving the stalwart Jeri home to man the phones, answer the unanswerable questions and generally assume the unspeakable: she may now be the oldest living child in the Southard family. Imagine THAT!

*   *   *

"I'm OK, Dad," Gary announced to me in a matter-of-fact voice, clearly his own. Actually, he announced it twice.

I have no doubt that I heard him say it. I would not swear to the exact time during the trip to the hospital that I heard this but when I think I heard it makes perfect sense to me.

The car ride to the hospital could only be described as nerve wracking, not because of Gary Tepe's driving but because I couldn't stand the delay in knowing and I couldn't stand the potential truth that kept floating into my consciousness despite my desperate attempts to submerge it. Diane continued to toss her calm reassurances back to me and I clung to them as surely as a drowning man clings to anything that floats.

"I'm OK, Dad," he said. When I think I heard him say it, we were passing a large field on the left hand side of Route 25 in Meredith. In the summer, the entire field is a mass of closely

planted corn stalks but as we passed it, just the miniscule shoots
of the plants were beginning to sprout from the black soil.

   I remember clearly that the first time I heard it, I sat up
straight, stunned by the realness of it. Then he repeated it.

   "I'm OK, Dad," as clearly as if he were sitting next to me. A
quick glance at Diane and Gary in the front seat confirmed my
suspicion that his words originated in my head. It was his voice;
there was no doubt in my mind. His reassuring words forced me
to sit up straight for the remainder of the trip, somehow sure that
when we arrived at the hospital, he would be fine.

   Now I know that I misinterpreted his message. His definition
of being OK was quite different than mine.

*   *   *

Emergency rooms in hospitals have always struck me as busy
places. Even when there are no patients in sight, the staff seems to
be in a hurry. I had a precise image of what this one was going to
look like, even down to the room where I would find my son with
a tube or two stuck in his arm and his wide smile telling me in person that he was indeed OK.

   Before the car rolled to a complete stop, I opened the door. I
jogged through the parking lot, leaving my friends far behind. The
automatic door slid open well before I arrived at the threshold, as
though welcoming me in. I glanced back and forth, to the right and
the left, and saw Pam in a small waiting room behind the nurses'
station. There was no sign of Barbara and I was sure I would find
her with Gary. Without asking permission from the nurse behind
the desk, I proceeded directly to Pam. The simple question I asked
remains with me even today.

   "What's going on here?" I asked, expecting to be directed to
Gary's room and Barbara.

   Pam's eyes filled and I remember saying something like "He's
OK, right?" Then the words tumbled out, each phrase more devas-
tating than the last. Even had I been recording her words right then,
I know I would never have gotten them right. When the message is

so jarring, so incredible, so absolutely unbelievable, we listen to the first sentence rather than simply hearing it. All that follows may be heard but listening becomes more difficult with each word. Everything that comes after the initial blow becomes a frenzied search through the debris of words for something positive, sifting through the bits and pieces of information like a miner panning for gold. I know I heard the word "flatline" in her first sentence but expected it to be followed by "revived" or "resuscitated" or some equally hopeful medical term. Instead, her ever-increasing tears mixed with a litany of phrases like "couldn't get him back" and "worked for almost an hour."

As Pam finished with a desolate (and this remains with me as well) "I can't believe this is happening, Daddy," I lost any semblance of control and put my head on her shoulder and wept.

I've often wondered what makes people stop crying in situations like this. What is there other than exhaustion that makes the tears dry up? Is there a physiological reason, a reservoir that simply runs dry and needs to be replenished? By the time my tear supply was depleted, Diane and Gary had arrived and stood in the middle of the emergency room, waiting. I felt the need to greet them but had no idea what would happen after the words left my mouth.

"He's gone," I told them as the environment turned surreal. Barbara, now a mom who had lost her first-born child, joined us and we all stood there in a tight cluster, wordlessly. The staff stayed at a distance as though a crowd control rope encircled our group. I'm not sure how much time passed before we dispersed; likely it was just a matter of a minute or two.

*   *   *

"It was a wonderful day," Barbara writes.

"After our nine holes of golf, we stopped at a take out place to satisfy Gary's craving for a lobster roll. When we got home, he started his stuffed shells and his special broccoli cauliflower salad as I acted as his sous chef. After Nan and Gary left for her doctor's

appointment, I showered and prepared to baby-sit for Ryan and Dex while the girls had their nails done. I was blow-drying my hair when the call came. Pam answered the phone and shakily called for me to answer it."

"With an amazing display of presence of mind, Nan asked a passer-by to call our home, even remembering our phone number under extremely stressful conditions. The woman said there had been an accident and they were applying CPR to Gary."

"Pam and I left immediately. Jeri stayed home to watch the boys. Driving through Moultonboro, we knew if we were speeding we would be stopped. The local police are notorious for their patrols in that section and sure enough we were soon pulled over. I hailed the police car and he had me get in the cruiser and sped off, leaving Pam behind to find her own way in our car."

"When we arrived at the hospital, I was escorted into a small private room which I thought at the time was odd. I expected to be told to wait in the room with all the others who had patients in the emergency room They wouldn't let me see Gary because, the nurse explained, the doctors were still working on him. I went to see my mother and she said that Gary had just collapsed at the wheel and she had checked his pulse but couldn't get one. Soon after, a doctor came in and announced that they couldn't save Gary."

The doctor represented the antithesis of the compassionate reaction of every other staff member in the emergency room. If ever a time called for a demonstration of a sympathetic bedside manner, this would seem to me to be it. Instead, the doctor, who shall remain nameless for obvious reasons, assumed a confrontational approach with a mother who had just lost her only son.

"His attitude was rather abrasive and questioning," Barbara says. "He said we 'must have known that Gary had heart problems' as though we could have made a difference. When Gary was a junior in high school, his usual sports physical showed a heart murmur. Because he wanted to go to West Point, we had a complete heart examination with a well-known specialist in Boston. My mind was frozen, locked in freeze frame mode. I couldn't even

think of the year he graduated from West Point or the year he had the heart exam. It simply wouldn't work. The doctor continued to question me and wasn't in the least empathetic. I'm a very emotional person and I knew that Pam would be arriving soon. I knew I had to be really strong because here she was preparing for her wedding just two days away and now she would also be dealing with the loss of her beloved brother."

"Pam arrived and while we were going over what had happened, the doctor left. Then I knew that Duke would be coming and he and Gary always had a special bond. I knew he would be really devastated so I just knew I was going to have to the strong one through all of this."

She was.

* * *

Barbara's strength rarely wavers. I know that she would not tolerate a lack of professionalism on the part of those whose most important responsibility is to alleviate pain and suffering, whether it is physical or emotional. When she told me about the attending doctor's actions after Gary's death, I was at first astounded but soon simply disappointed, wondering how he could have been so callous. The reality was that she was reeling and couldn't have reacted to his unprofessional behavior in her usual fashion. What I now understand is that she knew what had to be done, in spite of the harshness of the situation.

We approached one of the nurses and asked to see our son, needing but not really wanting some degree of confirmation. It was only then that I realized that Barbara had not been with Gary but with her mother when I arrived. The nurse, well trained and demonstrating the compassion required to work in a hospital emergency room, quickly agreed with the proviso that we give her time to "clean him up."

Only a string of clichés could describe my reaction to those words. "Gut-wrenching" and "heart-breaking" come immediately to mind. As we waited, we asked Pam if she wanted to go in with us and once again her eyes filled as she reluctantly said that she really couldn't. I understood perfectly, my knees already watery in anticipation.

Daddies are supposed to protect their daughters from pain and harm and I felt absolutely helpless. Putting Band-Aids on a little girl's skinned knee or tending to a bee sting doesn't quite compare with helping a grown daughter deal with her brother's death two days before her wedding.

The nurse came to us in just a few minutes and asked us to follow her. My watery knees began to shake and I prayed for the hand of God to help us get through this. I'm not sure what I expected but what I saw was our son asleep on a gurney. The bright overhead lights had been turned off and the soft glow of ambient light filtering through the door created a grayness in the room. I walked over to him, touched his forehead and ran my hand through his hair. My reservoir had been replenished; this time, the dampness simply overflowed and drizzled down my cheeks. How do parents say goodbye to a son who was no longer there? We stayed a minute or so. Then, it was simply too much. I wish I could remember saying a prayer before we left.

I can't.

*   *   *

Two other times I stood over Gary while he slept and gently rubbed his head. There were other times, I'm sure, but these included the added ingredient of a father's deepest emotion.

Precocious and intelligent little boys between the ages of two and three frequently test the patience of the parents as they navigate the turbulent terrible twos. Gary certainly fit the description of a toddler who found many different ways to make his parents sometimes feel as if they were bearing the trials of Job. The firstborn, especially if it is a son, carries a special burden, the burden of expected perfection on the part of his parents. This combination, a headstrong little boy and unrealistic parental expectations, led to one of the head rubbing incidents.

For whatever reason, long forgotten now, Gary had disrupted a family dinner gathering we were having with friends. I recall removing him from the dinner table and putting him in his crib with a light spanking. He was about two and a half at the time. Of course, he cried. Children in situations like these cry not so much from the pain of the harmless taps that parents give. I'm convinced that they cry from the humiliation of being embarrassed in front of others.

After I made several trips into our friends' bedroom to admonish him for his continual crying to come out with us again, he finally fell asleep, exhausted from his sobbing. After a time, when there was nothing but silence coming from the bedroom, I slipped in and looked down at him, the picture of innocence as he slept.

How could I have been so mean to him? He is just a little boy, I thought.

I felt my eyes moisten as I gently rubbed his head and wondered what his last thoughts were before he fell asleep. I hoped he would forgive me.

*   *   *

In the five years we had owned Beaver Hollow Campground, Gary was the stalwart worker. An uncertain venture at best, financial realities forced us to work the campground without hiring outside help, using our children to fill in whenever possible. Gary always was up for any task, whether it be collecting the trash or emptying a recreational vehicle's septic refuse. A strong, athletic build and self-motivation made him a valuable asset as we tried valiantly to make our enterprise work.

I've always believed that parents have their children until about age twelve or thirteen and then get them back at age twenty-two. In between, the first hope is that what happened before they left us emotionally, if not physically, is strong enough to help them through the extremely difficult adolescent years. The second hope is that they will come back.

Gary, a strong-willed adolescent, typically maintained his personal opinion on how things should be done around the campground. With all the naturalness of human nature, they occasionally clashed with ours.

One hot summer evening when he was a junior in high school, a disagreement over something long since forgotten escalated into an acrimonious argument. As so often happens with parent-teenager arguments, this one ended with Gary being sent to his room. At the campground, being sent to his room meant being sent to our room since the whole family slept in a single large room above the store and office. This was a particularly strong argument, the kind that makes fathers cringe later when they realize what horrible things they might have said in the heat of the moment.

Grudgingly and under extreme duress, Gary retired to his (our) room, much earlier than his usual bedtime. Later, when the busyness of the evening subsided, I went upstairs and found him sound asleep. My anger had drained out of me from its sheer negative weight.

I sat down on the edge of his cot and reached out to his forehead. Here was a really good kid. I was a high school teacher; every day I saw students who made me wonder how their parents ever dealt with them or the problems I was certain they presented on a daily basis. I knew how lucky we were. Yet I knew that I had hurt him that night.

I rubbed his head and he roused out of his sleep. I remember telling him how sorry I was and I hoped that his grogginess didn't interfere with his understanding the apology. The darkness of the room was a blessing; he couldn't see my eyes watering.

*   *   *

"He's only twenty nine years old, for God's sake!" I almost shouted when we reached the foyer of the emergency room. The loud exclamation attracted the attention of the several nurses in the area and I felt the color rise in my cheeks. I turned and gazed out the window while Barbara and Pam went to see Nan in an adjoining room.

A few minutes later, the nurse wheeled Nan out into the foyer of the emergency room. I'm sure I stared at her, my eyes demanding some sort of answer.

"What in heaven's name happened, Nan?" I asked, probably with considerable impatience. When no answer was forthcoming, I recall looking at her more closely, struck by how old she suddenly appeared. Only after the excruciatingly long car ride home did I realize that I had never even inquired about her condition. It is amazing how the trauma of death can make one forget even the most basic of courtesies. Here was my always-supportive mother-in-law in what had to be the most difficult situation of her life and I hadn't even asked how she was. What an absolute jerk!

Acting on instinct, Pam numbly retrieved our car while the rest of us waited in a daze at the door. We helped Nan out of the wheel chair into the car and soon the four of us were on the same road as the ambulance had traveled just a short time before. There was only silence for at least the first few miles as each of us groped through the dense fog of unbelieving shock. Nan sat quietly in the back seat, lost in thought. Many times since, I've tried to imagine what she must have felt as she searched for Gary's pulse immediately after the accident. Her physician's training had to tell her that her beloved grandson was gone. Perhaps her mind was replaying the whole scene during our ride home. Whether by design or by accident, she was excluded from the conversation. I think none of us could bear asking her to share any more of the details just yet. Eventually, several miles into the trip, the unique problem solving ability that is built into our human nature came to the surface.

What are we going to do now? Inevitably, the question had to be asked and who better than the bride-to-be and her parents to make the decision? The choices were clear. Either we postpone the wedding, now only forty-eight hours away, or we proceed. The discussion evolved into a series of plusses and minuses, the reasons for going ahead with the plans eventually outweighing the possibility of cancellation. We knew that many of Pam and Andy's friends in the military had planned leave time around the wedding and some of them already were on their way to New Hampshire. Central New Hampshire is not exactly on the way to anywhere and many of our friends were traveling long distances as well. Ultimately, the discussion moved into a more nebulous area, the necessarily obscure question of "What would Gary want?"

*   *   *

The "hail and farewell" soiree as assignments for Army commanders at all levels are changed is a long-standing tradition. One of these socials happened to coincide with one of our visits to Colorado Springs where Gary was stationed at Fort Carson. Heidi and Gary, always the most gracious of hosts, asked for and received permission to include us. At this party, I met Colonel Joseph Yakovac, Gary's commanding officer for the first time.

Parents from the beginning of time in every culture live for those times when their children make them proud. I have no doubt that the Neanderthal father's heart swelled with pride as he watched his son successfully hunt down his first animal. The pride I felt after Colonel Yakovac's unsolicited opinion of our son approached the feeling I had watching him receive his diploma and commission at West Point in 1984.

The colonel's description of Gary as the epitome of the West Point officer touched us immeasurably. While many view West Point as a rather harsh environment with little space for compassion, those who survive the grueling four years training to be officers would disagree. As one of the West Point chaplains pointed out in a brilliant sermon we were fortunate enough to have heard, West Pointers are the "peacemakers" from the Sermon on the Mount. The great general Douglas MacArthur himself believed that no one hates war more than a soldier for who has more to lose in war than the warriors fighting the battle.

Colonel Yakovak's description of Gary as an officer who ge-nuinely cared for his soldiers while effectively commanding them was confirmed in a written evaluation Gary forwarded to me in June of 1991.

In part, the evaluation read ". . .Never passes the buck nor will his officers or soldiers. Everything he does is for his company, never for self-gratification."

* * *

Gary would have wanted the wedding to go on, we finally decided after conferring with Jeri when we arrived home. Much of our discussion centered on the groom, Andy Lohman, and his family. Andy, we knew, already was in transit. His parents also planned to leave on Thursday so they too were almost to New Hampshire. I have come to realize that many human decisions are made based upon the immediate rather than the long term. In so many cases, motivation for the decision is driven by consequences that usually are in the near future. What if we postponed the wedding? Think of all the people who would be inconvenienced. The fact is that in four days most of those inconvenienced would be immersed in their lives again, giving the events in New Hampshire only an occasional backward glance.

I thought of that Robert Frost poem about the young boy who suffers a fatal accident while farming. Those who come to offer condolences are truly grief-stricken but soon afterward, because they are not "the one dead" things must move forward as they had planned. As bizarre as all this was, there was a blatant reality clouding the sky, a sky that felt as though it had a suffocating, one hundred foot ceiling. It was oppressive but at the same time enervating in light of the circumstances. It is amazing how reality intrudes on surreal situations and this assumed that quality. The wedding had to be made a reality, something sane in the midst of all the madness.

As we sat on the screened-in back porch late in the afternoon, the warmth of the May day did nothing to warm the enveloping coldness in our hearts. Nan, who had retreated to her apartment over our garage immediately upon our return home, came back over to our house in fifteen minutes, her plaintive "I just don't want to be alone" causing the tears to flow yet again.

There would be long periods of silence, interrupted by a single, simply-stated memory. Diane and Gary had taken Jeri's two boys home with them to use their hot tub. The thoughtful gesture left just the Southard family and Nan sitting around the porch, joined by a forever-empty chair.

"We never did the family picture," Jeri said at one point, emotion choking off the last word. The plan was to use the occasion of this family event to gather everyone for a portrait for posterity. At the time, I wondered if any of us would ever want to pose for another family photo.

The stuffed shells that were to be the dinner that night occupied most of the bottom shelf of the refrigerator, a bowl filled to overflowing with lifeless reminders staring up at anyone who might open the door. The ritual of our favorite cocktails was followed but the manhattans, usually potent appetite enhancers, couldn't overcome the connection between the shells and their source. There would not be any takers for Gary's specialty that evening. During our dazed cocktail hour, Pam spent much time on the phone alerting as many of her friends as she could and we felt we needed to do the same.

Barbara made the dreaded call to our best friends, Irene and Jerry Gares, in New Jersey. After a draining few minutes of sympathy running to empathy followed by the raw intensity of feeling that is only shared with loving friends, they assumed the responsibility of notifying everyone who was attending the wedding from that area. Speaking with friends and family at a time like this creates ambivalent feelings at best and resounding emotional clashes at worst. With their usual perception, Irene and Jerry knew that they could relieve some of that burden and we are forever grateful for that.

In our small town, word of any tragedy assumes a life of its own and soon after the call to Irene and Jerry, the parade of friends began. Each visit produced the expected highs of sensing the sincere desire of people wanting to share our pain coupled with the crushing lows of reality, the absolute truth that the unimaginable had really happened.

The evening became a blur, the hollow sensation in my stomach deepening with each visitor, a sensation not unlike hunger, except that it could not be satisfied, not with stuffed shells, not with manhattans and shrimp cocktail, not with anything on this planet. I wanted my son back.

Several of Pam's old friends had come over and they were enjoying the wonderful companionship that comes with youthful reunions, tempered as it was by the unexpected cloud of the day's events. For tiny fractions of time, all seemed well; the reminiscences flowed and laughter filled the room. About nine o'clock that night, Barbara and I went upstairs to bed, certain that the visits for the night were over but with no idea what kind of rest we might be able to get.

The crunch of tires on the stone driveway came shortly after. I selfishly hoped that it was another of Pam's friends, the thought of greeting another caller hollowing out my churning stomach once more. After the knock on the front door and the sound of muffled voices drifting up the stairs, Pam's voice called to us.

"It's Mr. Urda, Dad."

The emptiness deepened. The last time I saw the principal, my old friend and colleague, was the afternoon before as he greeted Gary in the Main Office at Kennett in his typically booming good-natured voice. That scene, so vivid and such a perfect picture of the conviviality that captured the two personalities, flashed through my mind as I hastily pulled on a pair of sweat pants and a tee shirt. I was shaking when I reached the bottom of the stairs.

Larry had been at an educational conference all day and only became aware of what had happened when our assistant principal called him. His unique, friendly habit of addressing me by my real name somehow made his greeting all the more poignant.

"Oh, Albert, I am so sorry," he said and we embraced in mutual sobs. Thankfully, he was the last caller of the night; I'm not sure how I could have handled another.

Chapter Two
Heaven- Sunday
Mothers' Day
May 10, 1992

Sir John Browning once said that "a happy family is but an earlier heaven." I would have to add the proviso that it is only an earlier heaven if it is not taken for granted. A quirk in human nature appears to be the notion that we are doomed to squander precious moments but I refuse to believe that we do this intentionally. Most of the time it is simply because we don't even recognize them. We would have difficulty recognizing them even if they were handed down to us as the tablets were presented to Moses. My guess is that we don't see them because they are so *ordinary*, so commonplace that they only stand out in hindsight.

*   *   *

I actually taught a course for several years in the early seventies with the Madison Avenue title of "Dead Is A Four Letter Word." The clever title was designed to entice students to choose it from a myriad of elective courses offered by the English Department. The "Phase Elective Program" provided a trendy substitute for the old fashioned English I, II, III and IV. Our department was convinced that this program would have a dramatic positive impact on our entire student body and certainly on the "less interested" and poorly motivated students. Predictably, the adolescent fascination with death filled the course rosters and I was faced each semester with more than fifty students eager to learn more about this universal blight on humanity.

A favorite unit of the students, and mine as well, was a short one on recognizing "precious moments" before they are gone. It was a unit filled with gripping stories of individuals regretting the unappreciated precious moments with loved ones just before a whole gamut of potential calamities befell them. Inevitably, the class discussion would come to the same conclusions. We have to live; we can't hibernate and let the world go by. If we didn't live life to the fullest, there wouldn't be any precious moments.

Gary lived life to the fullest but the precious moments we shared that week are as ephemeral as Marley's ghost was to Scrooge, apparitions that dissipate like our misty breath on a cold morning.

*   *   *

The situation bore a strong similarity to Christmas with one major exception; the anticipation of Christmas is more exciting than the actual event. My personal "week from Heaven" would, I was certain, far surpass the anticipation. Pam's wedding was scheduled for Saturday, May 16, and her arrival ten days before was just the start of the excitement. The real week from Heaven would begin when all three of our children were together.

We enjoyed the time with Pam by herself immensely and I savored the thought of the dinner table conversations with the three siblings contending for parental attention.

"Just like the good old days," I recall thinking on more than one occasion.

Adult brothers and sisters seem to take great pleasure in shocking their poor parents with tales of their younger days, each remembering the same events differently and. usually playing a bit of "one up-manship." The two girls especially welcomed any chance to cast their older brother in a devilish light. I looked forward to a whole week of the light-hearted and good-natured joshing. The days of the occasionally intense, omnipresent sibling rivalry were over, gradually disappearing as maturity placed its mark on family relationships.

*   *   *

"I never imagined I'd be left to sort through my mixed emotions and memories of the sibling rivalry we shared growing up," Jeri writes. "I never thought I'd be left alone to realize the resentment I

had harbored was all in vain, futile in the wake of his untimely death."

* * *

Gary's trip east for Pam's wedding was the beginning of an adventure, one that would reach far beyond his week of leave time at home. He had driven from his home in Colorado Springs to Kansas City where he would undertake yet another advanced officers' training school before attending the Colorado School of Mines in September, hoping to earn a Master's Degree in civil engineering. His career as an Army captain at Fort Carson had been exemplary and he was ready to move on to larger challenges. His plan included leaving his car on the base in Kansas City, flying home for the wedding and then returning on the Sunday after the wedding to his school.

His major regret, expressed at regular intervals during the week, was that his wife, Heidi, could not accompany him. Long separations are a well-understood part of the life of a soldier and she endured them stoically but this trip was different. Final exams in a Master's Degree program and her demanding job required her presence in Colorado and Gary missed her terribly.

"I saw Clemens pitch, Dad!" Gary called up the steps. It was late Saturday night and Pam and Gary had just returned from the airport. His excitement was obvious, much of my Red Sox fanaticism having successfully brainwashed our children. It was no wonder that his first greeting, after a hurried "Hi!" was about the Red Sox star pitcher. The stopover in Kansas City coincided with a Red Sox visit for a weekend series and he managed to find a ticket and watched Roger Clemens pitch a sparkling game.

Pam had generously agreed to go to the airport, knowing that the late arrival was well past the old folks' bedtime. We had tried to stay awake but kept drifting in and out of a light sleep. We fumbled our way down the stairs to greet him and after a family hug, we were treated to a quick game summary and a description of the beautiful ballpark in Kansas City.

*   *   *

Attending a baseball game together has few rivals as a traditional "quality time" activity for fathers and sons. At eight years of age, Gary was in his first year of little league and I decided that this was a perfect time to take him to a Yankees-Red Sox game at Yankee Stadium. Although I suspect his interest in playing organized baseball was the result of some not-so-subtle parental pressure, he seemed to enjoy the experience in center field, a position that rarely saw much action at his young level. The long lulls of inactivity provided him with the chance to make interesting designs with his foot all around the dirt outfield, always with his back to home plate. When not creating dirt castles, he would search for other distractions, much to the chagrin of his coach.

I was convinced that a visit to Yankee Stadium would capture the essence of the game for him, sending him back to his team with a new perspective. Instead, the awesome environment of the stadium caught his interest more than the game. Much of our day was spent climbing to the highest and farthest points in the dramatic structure, the game (a lopsided victory for the Yankees anyway) becoming a secondary reason for our trip. The hot dogs, the popcorn, the huge crowd, the vivid and unique sights and sounds and smells of the ballpark made the impression, not the game itself. Now I know that the experience of seeing that game probably set in motion a life-long interest as a fan but the reality was that he really did not like playing baseball, despite serving his obligatory time in Little League, both in New Jersey and in New Hampshire.

*   *   *

I was envious but the lateness of the hour prevented a long discussion about it. After a brief chat about his flight and the trip in general, we retired, leaving Pam and Gary to close up for the night and, I'm certain, continue to trade stories about their lives in the military, both during and after West Point.

The week from Heaven had begun.

*   *   *

Barbara and I awakened to the noisy clang of pots and pans filtering through the kitchen door at the bottom of the steps. It was 6:30 on Sunday morning.

"What in the heck are they doing down there?" I asked, incredulous that the "kids" could be up so early after such a late night. I whispered a "Happy Mother's Day!" to Barbara and then stumbled down the stairs much as I had the night before, this time struggling to awaken instead of being aroused from drifting into sleep. When I pushed open the kitchen door, I was greeted with two cheerful smiles and the delightful aroma of Canadian bacon sizzling in a frying pan.

"Go on back to bed, Dad. We're just cooking Mom a special breakfast," Gary said. "It's eggs benedict, her favorite." They had managed to find a store open on the way home from the airport to buy the ingredients and were now busy preparing a sumptuous breakfast after, I discovered later, just a few hours sleep.

"I have a really good recipe for homemade hollandaise sauce," Gary said. "Mom will love it." They obviously didn't need my assistance and were clearly enjoying the role reversal. It was always Barbara who prepared the special meals whenever any of the children visited home.

The "special" breakfast set the tone for the entire first day of the week. Attendance at church on Sunday mornings is a firmly ingrained habit with us and this Sunday would be no exception. I'm afraid that we really didn't give our children much choice about joining us in worship. After all, what "child" could refuse a mother's request on Mother's Day? Our children have always been a profound source of pride for us and it was another chance to show them off and to have them share our meaningful Sunday morning ritual.

*   *   *

Christmas Eve, 1980
While holiday happiness tends to be romanticized, for Gary this Christmas was truly special. It would be his first extended leave from the intense pressure of his plebe year at West Point. He had not been home since entering the academy in July and as Christmas approached, his letters were increasingly full of reminiscences of Christmases past, always with the hint that we could perhaps duplicate some of those experiences. Some, of course, were easy. The shrimp-cocktail appetizer, the prime rib dinner and Yorkshire pudding topped off with one of Barbara's delicious homemade desserts were a given for Christmas dinner. The outside Christmas lights and wreaths, the traditional inside decorations on the fireplace mantle and the freshly cut tree were easily put into place. More difficult to supply was a snowstorm on Christmas Eve but good fortune ruled and a light powdery snow began falling just before the traditional early service led by the children of the Sunday School.

Gary had brought home his full dress uniform from West Point and was as anxious to wear it to the worship service as he had been to shed his dress grays in the car as soon as we left the confines of West Point. Describing the pride inherent in seeing him in that uniform is impossible, as is the pride in being in his company at church that evening. His memories of the ceaseless tension of being a lowly plebe, the tearful phone calls home, and the academic pressures faded for the moment, replaced by his feeling of self-satisfaction. He had made it this far and was proud to accept the adulation of our congregation. He was a West Point cadet.

The fluffy light snow swirled in an increasing breeze as we left the church. By early on Christmas morning, the temperature had fallen well below zero and a strong northwesterly wind rattled the windows. Another of his requests that we thought would be easy to

fill was to have a romantic fire in the fireplace on Christmas morn-
ing as we opened our gifts. I had set aside several "yule logs" for
the occasion, each large enough to burn most of the day. The
harsh, bitter cold normally would have prevented me from starting
the fire and watching the heat in the house disappear up the chim-
ney but before anyone came downstairs, I lit the fire. As expected,
the central fireplace immediately began sucking the heat from the
house and we shivered our way through the entire day, struggling
to keep the house warm. I'm glad I lit that fire but I certainly
didn't recognize it as a precious moment when I did it.

*   *   *

Special occasions like birthdays and Mother's Day in our household feature the celebrant's choice of meals and activities for the
day. Barbara, not surprisingly, wanted to play golf that afternoon
and we headed for the course immediately after lunch. The day
was topped off by a typical family cookout, replete with all the
standard foods and the stern admonition to Barbara that she wasn't
to lift a finger to help. This was her day.

That evening, as we sat on the deck sipping the celebratory
cocktails and hors d'oeuvres that always accompanied special occasions, we were discussing the various happy homeowner projects
that I planned on squeezing in between rounds of golf during the
upcoming summer vacation. There was nothing unusual about the
conversation at the time; it consisted mostly of family recollections
and jokes about my ineptitude as a handy man.

"If it can't be done with a screwdriver and hammer, we're out
of luck," Barbara was fond of saying. I mentioned that one of my
jobs was to repair the track on one of our overhead garage doors
that had gotten in the way of the car as I backed out several years
before. Gary made a harmless comment that meant nothing at the
time but would assume a life of its own in just a few days and continues to haunt me years later.

He assured us that he would fix the door since he was looking
for projects so he wouldn't be bored.

"I want to do something around here that will make you think of me every time you use it," he said. He began the repair but was unable to complete it. I can't even look at the door, much less use it, without thinking of him.

*   *   *

"We're putting in a hot tub on our deck and it needs reinforcing. How did you do that on your deck, Dad?"

The question began a Sunday phone call that had a purpose but what I missed most at first were the Sunday phone calls without a purpose, the kind with a few silences as we tried to think of things that were "new" in answer to the standard "What's new?" question. Unless he was on field maneuvers, we could be fairly sure of making some contact on Sundays. Even during his service in the Berlin Brigade in Germany, regular contact on Sundays bridged the communication gap quite well. The homeowner questions from the beautiful home in Colorado Springs came on an as-needed basis but the regular Sunday afternoon calls, with their comfortable silences, were what I missed.

Early on a Sunday afternoon during the winter before he died, I remember initiating the phone call. Heidi explained to me that he had earlier embarked on one of his spontaneous adventures. The proximity of Pike's Peak was a constant temptation, he had told me once. He really wanted to see what it would be like to bivouac on the mountain during a snowstorm. With an imposing storm predicted late Saturday afternoon, he and another officer under his command had set off to spend the night on the mountain after climbing as high as they could. Heidi informed me, a bit of nervousness in her voice, that they hadn't yet returned but they were expected any moment.

In the years we've lived in New Hampshire, I've lost two acquaintances to the treacherous winter conditions of Mt. Washington, known for the "worst weather in the world" because of its unique geographical location. I thought of a harrowing summer trip up the Pike's Peak auto road with Gary and I recall the im-

ages of both my professional colleague and a former student flashing through my mind, both dead because of the vagaries of a mountain in winter. People climbing Mt. Washington try to anticipate winter storms to avoid being caught in the unforgiving climate. Here were my son and a companion deliberately climbing a higher mountain with the expressed purpose of "enjoying" the approaching storm. I just shook my head and asked that he call me as soon as he came in. At eight o'clock that night, his exuberant phone call made me chuckle, first with relief than with admiration for his youth and vitality. I laughed out loud when he told me that I should have been there.

Now, I wish I had been.

Chapter 3
Heaven-Monday
May 11, 1992

Grudgingly and with no small degree of jealousy, I left the family behind on Monday morning. With Barbara working the first two days of the week, I asked my car pool partners if they would mind driving so that my car would be available for "the kids" to use. We left that morning sure that Gary and Pam would be making their own family memories for the beginning of her last few days as a single woman. The commonality of experiences at West Point and in the military had eliminated most of the naturally occurring problems in their sibling relationship, although they both were well aware that Gary still outranked her, as older brother and U.S. Army captain.

*   *   *

Gary admitted that his returns to West Point, even after he achieved the rank of captain, were not all that comfortable. Despite being saluted by the cadets and afforded the respect that came with his rank, the memories of the harshness of his four years there overshadowed the confidence inspired by his successful career. If his sister had not been there, I'm not sure that he would have returned until enough time had passed to allow the positive memories to outnumber the negative ones. While his loyalty was strong and his commitment deep, he often wondered how the "old corps" seemed to relish telling their war stories of life at the Point, as though the experience had been nothing but fun and frolic. I've always had the feeling that had he lived, he would have been at the forefront of storytellers at his twenty-fifth reunion.

His first return to West Point after graduation was a visit to Pam, one that included Jeri. I recall him telling me that he would be "dressing down" for the occasion, wearing civilian clothes to disguise his military connection so that he wouldn't be returning a cadet's salute a hundred times every block. His return for Pam's graduation would be an entirely different story.

*   *   *

I wasn't certain of all the plans in place for the day but I was sure the entire family would have a boundless list of happy memories from every day of this particular week. What I didn't know was that Gary would be "pulling rank" and enlisting Pam's assistance in working on the garage door project, the one that would make us think of him every time we used it. As Pam describes it, the transformation from comrades in arms back to big brother, little sister happened quickly that day. There was no question who would be in charge and a large part of the day was spent wrestling with the major project that I had managed to avoid. By the time I arrived home from school that day, the repair of the door remained in a state of flux, still needing a few obscure parts that the average person doesn't even know exist in their garage doors.

Diane and Gary Tepe hadn't met my son and as the car turned into the driveway, I asked them to come in to meet him. Before we were even out of the car, he had bounded out of the door, his usual wide smile greeting us. I noticed the garage door was open and he quickly explained that it was a work in progress. After a brief exchange of greetings, my car pool partners left and I followed him into the garage and listened to the saga of the door repair. By that time, Pam had joined us and added her commentary, including how sore her shoulders were from being the "assistant" who did the grunt work while the "boss" handled the finesse jobs. We had a few hearty laughs, mostly at Pam's expense, and Gary assured me that he would have the door in working order the next day.

*   *   *

Late Thursday night, I went out to pull the overhead door down. It was a dark, clear night, made even darker by the sadness squeezing my heart. The night sky in rural New Hampshire can be breathtaking on clear nights when the temperature is cool and the air is dry. Looking up at the millions of stars is humbling and under the right circumstances, can lead to some profound philosophical discussions and has on several occasions. As I reached for the handle of the door, I paused momentarily and let the canopy of light form as my eyes became accustomed to the dark. Then I pulled the door down. Since the repair was completed on Tuesday, the door had worked well- not perfect, but well. About one third of the way down, the heavy door came to a sudden stop. Gary's newly installed piece of track had shifted slightly and would not allow it to close. I vividly remember looking back to the sky and laughing amid the tears streaming down my face. I had the distinct impression that someone else was laughing with me.

*   *   *

When we first moved to Tuftonboro, a car passing our house was so unusual that we would rush to the window to see who it was. Obviously, time has changed that somewhat but for two world-wise army officers, weekdays in early May were not exactly exciting in our little town. After a pleasant evening of cocktails and dinner, Gary and Pam decided to see if anything was happening in the neighboring town of Wolfeboro, a much more cosmopolitan town with its burgeoning population of over three thousand people.

They spent most of their evening at the Back Bay Boat House, one of the few restaurants in town that had a lounge open on a Monday night. Like old Army buddies, they shared a few beers and any number of dart games.

Pam describes that evening as the night she realized that her "Big Brother" had become a friend.

*   *   *

Gary and Heidi were married during a freak warm spell in late December of 1984. The temperature soared into the fifties, wreaking havoc with the ski areas in New Hampshire and creating huge puddles of slush and water throughout the North Country.

One evening shortly before the wedding, our living room was filled with some of Pam's friends and several of Gary's fellow officers, including his former roommate at West Point, George Hluck. The conversation turned to where Pam might be going to college. Her choices included West Point, along with the politically-diametrically-opposed Brown University in Rhode Island. Much of the discussion centered on discouraging Pam from attending West Point should she have the opportunity. The former West Point cadets in the group were adamant about how difficult it was for anyone, especially if that one happened to be a woman.

Through a variety of circumstances, Pam finally settled on West Point and no one was prouder at her graduation than Big Brother Gary. It is Captain Gary S. Southard who appears in the pictures, pinning the Second Lieutenant bars on her right shoulder. It was Gary who hugged her with tears in his eyes as he congratulated her on her accomplishment. Most of the warnings of the hardships of a woman at West Point had been valid but she had weathered the adversities and he was elated. I like to think they became friends then, as they stood together as fellow officers in the United States Army.

Chapter Four
Heaven- Tuesday
May 12, 1992

The centerpiece of the agenda for the day was, yet again, the garage door repair. Another important item on Gary's "to do" list was a trip to see Jeri and the boys in Lebanon, Maine. The plan was to combine the search for the repair parts with the visit to see Ryan and Dexter, his two nephews who barely knew him. After an early morning visit with mother-in-law Marguerite in Moultonboro, he and Pam set off to Maine for yet another memory making trip, another of those precious moments that only become special when they become memories.

*   *   *

Jeri continues.

"I couldn't fit a trip to Tuftonboro into my busy life the week of the wedding. My two toddlers, plus a house, job and husband had every waking second filled to the brim. I knew there'd be plenty of time for visiting the following weekend, with all the stuff to do with the wedding. If it had not been for him, and his effort to visit me, I wouldn't have seen him before he died. I struggle to remember the last time I saw him before that Tuesday when he came to my house for a brief, but now precious visit. Was it Pam's graduation? The picture of him holding Ryan as a baby reminds me of that time. Had he ever seen Dex? I don't even remember. In a way, I'll never forgive myself for not making the time. . .for the Europe visit, the trip to Tuftonboro when he arrived in town, or simply, the time to forgive him for being my perfect older brother while he was living. I just always thought there would be a lifetime for that.

Sure, he was mean and spiteful when we were kids; what little sister could say anything different? I remember it now with a smile and mourn for the adult relationship we could have had."

* * *

This Tuesday, a common sort of day, typifies why I believe that Henry David Thoreau is incorrect when he says "the masses of men lead lives of quiet desperation." I believe that most of human existence is not quiet desperation. As people go about their every day lives, their sense is not one of desperation. Instead, I believe their sense is one of purpose. The desperation enters only when Fate supplies an experience that sends our sense of purpose skittering in shambles across the floor of life.

Think about this: there was no desperation on that Tuesday as we all set about our tasks for that day. If anything, the anticipation of the day created strong, positive energy in all of our lives. Nothing out of the ordinary occurred. The mundane and common are comfortable and most people would prefer that the perennial status quo not be upset. The desperation sets in when lives are disturbed, when events spiral out of our control.

Visiting with a sister and her children or making a household repair are well within our limits of control. Tuesday was just an ordinary day.

Chapter Five
Heaven-Wednesday
May 13, 1992

Gary had been given strict orders. I rode that morning in the car pool and he was to pick me up at Kennett immediately after school closed. It was another beautiful spring day filled with the excitement of doing something different. As the wedding neared, each day increased the anticipation but this was to be a special one. Golf was not one of Pam's favorite activities but she relented and agreed to play nine holes with us after school, probably because we extended the carrot of a dinner at Chequer's Villa, a wonderful local Italian restaurant.

Gary came to Conway to do some outlet shopping and arrived at Kennett before the final period was over. The assistants in the library had seen his picture on my desk for years but never met him. They fawned over him like schoolgirls. His military bearing and posture combined with his six feet, three-inch height to make him an imposing physical presence. I showed him a few new computer additions to the library and heard the whispered "Who is that?" questions from the ever-curious students as we circulated through the crowded facility.

With no classes reserving the library for that period, the students filling it were those who elected to escape from a study hall environment, each with his or her own reasons. We worked hard at making the library a welcoming place and its relaxed but controlled atmosphere did make it a popular location for study but for the final period of the day its central location was an added attraction. The routes to the school busses, the sports locker rooms and the cafeteria were much shorter from the library than most of the study halls located in classrooms in the outer reaches of the building. We had a core of "regulars" who were in the library every day during this period and almost a year of rapport with them resulted in friendly and warm greetings for Gary as we moved among the tables. With a minute or two remaining before the tone sounding the end of the school day, the usual rustling of papers and stuffing of backpacks began. I escorted Gary out the rear door, clearly labeled NOT AN EXIT, and to the main office before the hallways filled with exuberant students celebrating their survival of another day of tedium.

Larry Urda, a long time associate at Kingswood Regional High School, had been the principal of Kennett since 1988, the year I arrived there. I likely would not have been offered the position if Larry had not been the principal. My age, educational credentials and years of experience had derailed several other opportunities and were it not for our long and positive professional association, it seems unlikely that the Conway School District would have been any different.

I knew that Larry would enjoy seeing Gary. It had been years; I wasn't even sure how long. I also knew that the principal would be very visible in the central hallway outside the main office as school was dismissed. He always knew what was happening in every corner of his school and his presence permeated the building. His boisterous but sincere manner was well known to staff and students alike and I was not surprised when he acknowledged Gary loudly, shouting a cheerful greeting across the hall. We chatted for a full ten minutes before Gary mentioned our golfing date that afternoon.

"So what are you doing standing here?" I recall Larry asking. Mentioning the gorgeous weather, he quietly suggested that perhaps I could be released a bit early for the occasion. With that encouragement and the links beckoning, we were soon walking briskly through the parking lot toward the car.

The Indian Mound Men's Twilight League occupies the tee box at the course from three to five every Wednesday afternoon. I had either forgotten about it or simply didn't know but as soon as I saw the crammed parking lot, I knew we wouldn't be playing golf that afternoon. While some disappointments can be crushing, others are manageable and this certainly fell into the manageable category. After all, we would be playing on Friday, the day before the wedding, with several friends and family who were attending the event. It really wasn't the end of the world. Just the two of us might even be able sneak in another round early on Saturday while the girls and the mother of the bride were busy with hairdressers and manicurists and all those other women things on the day of a wedding. The other golfing opportunities in the near future easily negated my disappointment.

*   *   *

The intrusion of the real world into a child's life is painful sometimes and watching your child cry is never easy. The blunt, breathtaking disappointments of childhood are crushing, not matter how insignificant they might seem to the adults in a child's world. We never learn that everything is relative and everything is important to those who are experiencing it. To a little girl, the loss of a favorite doll is as important as the loss of a billion-dollar contract to a CEO of a large corporation. The experience is especially agonizing in either case when there is absolutely nothing that can be done about it.

*   *   *

In 1976, Barbara and I made a decision to purchase a campground with the optimistic hope that financial independence would eventually follow. We held several family meetings with the three children about what changes might occur in our summer lives since we would be living at the campground. Just as the romance of the idea had clouded my thinking, the children's reaction was based on the enjoyment we all had when we went camping. We loved camping so what could be better than owning a campground?

Gary's reaction was the most enthusiastic. As we explained that all of them would be involved in helping us operate it, he saw the opportunity to have a summer job for the foreseeable future. The girls were still at that age where they believed their parents must know best and agreed that it would be an adventure for them as well.

The morning of the day we were scheduled to make settlement on the property, Gary and I packed up our travel trailer and loaded our lawnmower into our station wagon. The owners, having lost interest in the property, had neglected the outside maintenance and happily gave permission for Gary to begin cutting grass around the property while we signed our future away at a bank in North Conway. His excitement when we dropped him off at the campground on our way to the settlement was palpable. He promised to have the front lawn finished before we returned as the new owners of Beaver Hollow Campground.

As adults, we tend to expect disappointments in life because we see the inevitability that they are lurking in everything we undertake. What transpired at the settlement was a bitter reminder of this truth. The seller's lawyer had failed to read the sales agreement until that day and in the car on the way to the closing, he recommended that the deal not be accepted unless we came up with what to us was an impossible amount of cash. This was announced to us before we had even settled into our chairs. A short time later, we were driving down Route 16, reeling from the disappointment but using every cliché in the book regarding how "everything happens for a reason" and "it wasn't meant to be."

As we turned into the driveway, I could see Gary still pushing the lawnmower between two of the sites on the first row. When he saw us, he turned off the mower and came running over. His broad smile announced the pride in his work. I got out of the car quickly and put my arm around his shoulder. I offered a brief explanation of what happened, one I'm sure he didn't really understand. As the reality washed over him, he put his head on my shoulder and the tears began to flow. I vaguely remember apologizing but mostly I remember the helplessness of seeing my sensitive adolescent son, a big boy ready to enter high school, experiencing a crushing disappointment and I was unable to do anything about it.

A week later, the campground deal had been reconstructed and
we were able to purchase it but I'll never forget Gary's disillu-
sionment that day. It broke my heart. Children shouldn't hurt be-
cause of the mistakes of their parents or other adults in their lives.

*   *   *

We left the golf course, sure that we could be home before Pam
and Barbara left to meet us for the round of golf that was not going
to happen. About halfway across the rough, frost-heaved road between Center Ossipee and Tuftonboro, we passed their car heading
in the opposite direction. Pam, well known in our family as being a
bit on the heavy-footed side, was driving and they went past in a
blur but not before we were able to signal them. After a mid road
meeting, we decided to go to a driving range on Route 16 then to
dinner at Chequers Villa as we had promised Pam in exchange for
enduring our round of golf. I looked forward to introducing Gary
and Pam to the excellent Italian restaurant owned by friends whom
we had met at the golf course.

For the three of us who played golf, the long practice session
with all of the typical golfers' kibitzing about this grip or that type
of club or which ball is best was thoroughly enjoyable. Pam, I'm
sure, simply suffered through it for our sake, waiting for the fine
meal we would be enjoying later.

Chequers Villa was the setting for our last family meal with
Gary. As Emily questions in Thorton Wilder's powerful play, *Our*
Town, why don't we humans appreciate our precious moments on
this earth when they are happening? Instead, when the chance to
savor them is long gone and their recovery is impossible, we re-
troactively lament allowing them to pass without really noticing
them. The dinner at Chequers, complete with fine food and discussions that ranged from politics (the presidential candidacy of Ross
Pirot) to the practical (the upcoming weekend with its exciting myriad of events) fits well into that unappreciated, still lamented category. In less than twenty-four hours, there would be a permanently
empty chair at our family dinners.

While Barbara and I usually retired early, Gary and Pam convinced us that we should pick up a movie to watch that night. We would pass the local video store on the way home and I could return the film during the morning commute. With four opinions, the selection of the film was difficult and finally, with the promise that "Mom can go to bed whenever she wants to," we settled on two films. Our children knew that I loved movies and could easily watch one or two every night if practicality didn't interfere.

Close to midnight, as the credits for the second film rolled by, Barbara announced that she was going to bed. "City Slickers", a hilariously funny film, was the second part of the video family double feature. In one of many poignant scenes played so well by Billy Crystal, the "slickers" are engaged in a difficult and soul-searching discussion about the best and the worst days of their lives. Crystal, as effective as ever, speaks of the day his abusive father finally left the family, never to return. Refusing to place the event in either category, he calls it both his best and his worst day. That particular scene is played beautifully and the entire film so affecting that Barbara postponed the enticing call of bedtime as we turned our attention to our own best and worst days. The spontaneous discussion lasted until almost one o'clock, when we could no longer ignore the realities of time. Tomorrow was another day.

Retrospection is such a wonderful place to visit. Looking backward eliminates all guesswork and now, thinking about that evening, I know that we were only talking about bad days and good days. It is not an earth-shattering truth but everything is relative, we decided. What is one person's worst day could be a high point is someone else's life. Failing a major exam, losing a girlfriend to a best friend or a fender bender accident all may be important but it's the familiar syndrome of feeling sorry for yourself because you have no new shoes until you meet a man who has no feet. Although the discussion of best and worst days remains a pleasant memory, I could not reconstruct it well enough to document each of our best and worst days. That is probably just as well considering what happened less than twenty-four hours later.. Human existence is such that each day has the potential of residing in either category, perhaps in both.

Pam and Gary finally permitted us to trundle off to bed. The usual five A.M. wake up call was looming. I didn't even take the time for the usual nightly hygiene, promising myself to brush an extra minute or two the next morning. After a brief good night kiss, I turned over, my head settling into the pillow filled with thoughts of a few of my most noteworthy bad days. I was asleep in minutes, thankfully not realizing that Thoreau's desperation was closer than I could have imagined.

*   *   *

The plebe year at West Point is a grinding test of emotional, physical, academic and psychological stamina. The week prior to the annual Army-Navy football game supplies a brief respite from the intensity as the rivalry draws attention of the Corps away from the lowly plebes. The fervent hope of every plebe is that the Army football team will win the always bitterly contested game as a win traditionally means that the plebes may "fall out" until Christmas break. To the hapless plebes, who were at the mercy of every upper classman, being able to fall out meant that they might attain almost human status for at least a few weeks between the game and Christmas. The humiliation of the plebes, a critical factor in the successful transformation of high school seniors into West Point cadets, would cease, at least for a short while. Unfortunately, in Gary plebe's year, the football team ran into a superb Navy team with an all-American halfback named Nate McCallum and was soundly trounced. As I joked about returning to the grind the next day, I had no idea of the depth of disappointment nor did I imagine how much it meant to be able to "fall out."

The next morning, as we packed up our car and prepared for the trip back, the clowning, laughter and good times of the night before were replaced with a subdued resignation. Gary had always said that only a few "like" West Point; most of the cadets simply tolerate it. The training and tradition and pressure and stress are appreciated only later when their careers prove its effectiveness in preparing them for the leadership roles they all must assume.

The conversations in the car during the two-hour ride back to the barracks gradually dwindled until there was complete silence for the last twenty minutes or so. The plebes were to report in by noon on Sunday and we arrived at West Point at eleven thirty. We parked as close to Gary's barracks as possible. After unloading their gear and several food-stuffed care packages left over from the weekend, we watched as he and one of his friends made their way toward "home" like reluctant schoolboys returning to school after a long vacation. They already were acknowledging the upper classmen with the required "sir" greeting and salutes.

Ten minutes later, Gary returned, looking quite spiffy in his uniform, I thought. His face had the familiar, pinched look of someone under duress. The hugs and goodbyes were quick as he had to report in. As he hugged Barbara, I saw over her shoulder that his eyes were filled and my throat tightened. At moments like those, a parent needs to be strong but I felt like telling him to get in the car and come home with us. It was then that I realized how disappointing the loss the previous day had been and regretted making light of it. I was the last of the family to receive the hug and I recall feeling the need to say something brilliant to make things easier for him. All I could come up with was an inane remark about Christmas coming fast. His response was a muffled "yeah" and he turned away. I'm sure he was slightly embarrassed by the boyish tears but to me, his sensitivity was endearing, just as it had been at the campground that day four years before.

"Thanks for everything," he said as he spun on his heels and strode toward the barracks, already exhibiting the bearing and presence of a West Point cadet. We watched as he squared the corner at the barracks and disappeared into the harsh life of a West Point plebe.

Chapter Six
Hell- Friday
May 15, 1992

Students in my American Literature classes would often accuse me being wildly biased, spending large chunks of class time on the "Belle' of Amherst" while more significant poets occupied considerably less time. I willingly pled guilty to their charges but not without what I saw as valid reasoning. Most deaths send survivors on a fruitless search for answers and the wasteful death of our son, so stunning and so unreal, did the same to me. At some point during the restless night on Thursday, a poignant Emily Dickinson poem formed in my head.

> "The Bustle in a house
> The morning after death
> Is solemnest of industries
> Enacted upon earth,---
> The sweeping up the heart,
> And putting love away
> We shall want to use again
> Until Eternity."

In just a few words in a single poem, she captures the desolation of loss but juxtaposes the devastation with the hope of sweeping up the love and keeping it until we can use it in eternity, a clear implication in her belief that we all shall indeed meet again.

I believe that the poem came to life soon after we spoke with Heidi. At two o'clock in the morning, the phone rang. We could not say we were truly awakened by it because any sleep we had thus far had been fitful at best, interrupted by searing memories of the previous day. Barbara's mumbled hello was followed quickly by her jolting upright in bed. From her response and the sadness lurching across her face, I knew it had to be Heidi.

At various times during the evening before, I had tried to picture where our daughter–in–law might be as she trekked across the country from Colorado, alone on an airplane. My mind tried unsuccessfully to focus on the scene at her office when she received the terrible phone call from her mother, just another surreal scene in the ongoing tragedy.

Heidi's question was short and I knew from Barbara's response that it likely was just a simple "What happened?" I listened once again to the familiar story of the afternoon, surprised at Barbara's strength as she related the details. The conversation ended with the promise that we would be over to her mother's house with our pastor the next morning. Barbara gently put the phone down and turned off the light.

"How's she doing?" I remember asking, at the same time realizing how utterly stupid the question was. It became a rhetorical question, hanging in the air, answered only by a muffled sob. Then we returned to the vain attempt at sleep.

*   *   *

Barbara and I spent a sleepless night, only occasionally dozing then awakening to an unreality of what we both believed simply had to be just a bad dream. Finally in desperation, we decided to get up and go for a long walk despite the 5:30 a.m. hour. It was the first full day of our lives after Gary's death.

About two hundred yards from our driveway on Mountain Road, a quiet country road turns toward Canaan Valley. It is the road that Gary had run the morning before as he had done on countless other occasions. As we approached the intersection, I noticed a golf ball in the road, sitting virtually in the center of Canaan Valley Road where it joined with Mountain Road. Curious, I retrieved the ball from its most unlikely location and looked at it more closely. The memory that swept over me raised the hair on the back of my neck. The prickling continued as I turned the ball over in my hand.

"I still have an old Waukewan golf ball, Dad. Can you believe that?" Gary had said earlier in the week as he searched though his golf bag before we stepped on the first tee at Indian Mound. The summer before we played at Waukewan and he had bought several logo balls at the pro shop.

The Waukewan logo emblazoned across the golf ball blurred as I looked down at it in my shaking hand. In the next irrational moment, I tossed the ball into the woods, an action I have regretted ever since. I've thought since then about looking for the ball in the forest but I'm not sure what I would do if I found it. I'm not even sure what it means, if anything. I'm sure that it is just another coincidence.

The next time I saw a golf ball carrying a Waukewan logo was on a busy day at our course, over nine years afterward. It was lying in plain sight on the edge of a small pond, as if placed there. With the number of golfers passing by the pond that day, I was quite surprised to see a ball that surely should have been picked up by someone ahead of us. I retrieved the ball and looked around, expecting to see another golfer in pursuit of his errant ball but there was none. I looked at more closely, noticing the new condition as I rolled it in my hand. That Waukewan ball now resides in a special small pocket of my bag, a reminder of another coincidence years before. I have no plans to ever use it.

* * *

The long walk down the "valley road" helped to clear the fuzziness left over from the sleepless night but did nothing to alleviate the searing grief. Any attempt to capture in words our state of mind is as elusive as trying to describe a neighborhood viewed from an interstate highway at seventy-five miles per hour. The emotion of disbelief and denial was so powerful that grim reality intruded only a few times, occasions when we would stop walking and cling to each other in desperation. The entire walk was uninterrupted by any passing automobiles, the few residents living on the lonely country road not yet up and about.

A little more than a mile down the road, there is a small estate that the owner has aptly named "Quietude." On many of our walks before and since, Quietude was our destination, far enough and with sufficient hills to provide a solid exercise workout. That morning, we turned around to come home just before reaching it, the serenity surrounding Quietude clashing with the churning upheaval in our hearts and minds. The sun had already risen, splashing the mountains but not yet dispersing the cool air that settled in the hollows overnight. The early spring morning promised a spectacular day to follow but neither of us could bring ourselves to mention the change that had occurred in our plans for this day. The golf, the rehearsal dinner, the arrival of a sizable contingent of New Jersey friends and relatives and all the other exciting events of a day preceding a wedding in the family had been replaced by pastor's calls, cemetery visits, and gut-wrenching "sweeping up of love."

Pam was already awake and in the kitchen when we returned. I am always amazed at what creatures of habit we are and how, even in the face of harsh and unrelenting sadness, we continue to go through the motions of life. We made a desultory attempt at normalcy by preparing breakfast but there was no chance for anything to be considered normal that day. A phone call from our pastor, Russ Petrie, confirmed that he would accompany us to visit Heidi at her mother's condominium and he arrived at our house an hour later.

Russ's sentimentality is incongruous with his physical appearance. He is a burly man with a commanding presence yet easily moved to tears during emotional parts of church services. As soon as he entered our house, he enfolded us in strong hugs, squeezing yet another round of tears from each of us. In these situations, clergymen are expected to have answers where there can be none, solutions where there are none and soothing consolation when it is impossible to comfort. Although his compassion and understanding were obvious and all the right words were said, the desolation remained. I've wondered, both before and since, if pastors realize the hopelessness of trying to bring any level of comfort in these situations.

When the inevitable discussion of the "arrangements" began, the surreal world of disbelief descended on me again. When people hear of a death, one of the first questions always has to do with the arrangements, as in "What are the arrangements?" This always seems to me like the seating chart at a wedding is being discussed. I believe that the final disposition of a human being is the only experience that comes close to matching sports events for the overuse of euphemisms and clichés. The single phrase that is the least bit hopeful is referring to the body of a recently deceased as the "remains." That euphemism at least implies that there was more to the person than his physical substance; a soul, perhaps?

We informed Russ that the wedding would go on as scheduled and we would discuss everything else with Heidi when we visited that morning. I tried to picture that visit and I couldn't imagine facing her. Like the many colors of the rainbow, human emotions may also form a complex spectrum and the first time that a person greets a friend, relative or even a distant acquaintance after a loved one dies, the whole range is exposed. The interaction of two levels of grief allows for each to feed off the other and the depth of emotion is never matched again in subsequent meetings. Each succeeding time becomes easier, as if a barrier had been smashed. It may now be examined in the rear view mirror instead of head-on. The impact of that first meeting recedes ever quicker in the mirror with each passing day. But, as anyone who drives a modern automobile well knows, objects seen in the rear view mirror may be closer than they appear.

*   *   *

Our dear friends, Kathy and Dean Mendenhall and their son Jesse were three-quarters of the way through fulfilling their dream of a year long cruise on their sailboat when Gary died. Dean wrote a wonderful letter, saying in part how Gary was "someone to be proud of and he accomplished much while he was with us. The fact that you had a good son, thought a lot of him and were close is a blessing in itself, as you must know." We did.

It was early August when I drove past their house. We had missed them terribly and I was quite anxious to see them, despite the twinge of nervousness caused by the awareness of the difficult "first time" syndrome. They had expected to be home late the day before and as I approached their house, I saw Jesse, our godson, riding his bike down the country road. I turned into their driveway. The three months since Gary passed had seen a decrease in the jarring memories that would wash over me, catching me by surprise and feeling like physical slaps in the face. I was in complete control as I threw my arm around Jesse's shoulder and we walked into the house. He went to his parent's room and I heard him call, "Uncle Duke's here!"

I hadn't seen them for a year, enough of a reason for an emotional greeting, but I wasn't prepared for the power that a twenty one-year friendship held for me. The sight of their faces overwhelmed me and I sobbed in their arms as our first meeting took its place among the host of others in the rear view mirror of life. I recall how wonderful I felt after seeing them and I realized what a powerful healing force those first time meetings could be.

* * *

Heidi's brother greeted us at the door. His eyes were red and puffy, a clear result of a sleepless and difficult night. Eliot was a former student of mine and I have the greatest respect and admiration for him as a West Point graduate with an outstanding career in the military. After the initial greetings and introductions to Russ, he posed the universal question for the clergy. I can recall exactly how he phrased it.

"So, do you have any answers?" he asked.

The question came from his heart and was not meant to be flippant in any way. The edge of desperation was obvious as it is whenever anyone is searching for answers that are not going to be forthcoming. We had discussed the close relationship that Gary had with Eliot on the way to the house so Russ was not surprised by the depth of bitterness wrapped around the question. Marguerite sat on the sofa wringing a well-dampened handkerchief in her hand, her head bowed. Before Russ had a chance to answer, Heidi appeared in the hall, drawing all of our attention.

*   *   *

Heidi and Gary had been "buddies" throughout most of their high school years. The appellation of "buddies" covered their relationship well, although as parents we suspected that by their senior year, the term encompassed much more than its general definition. The four years of college for Heidi and West Point for Gary necessitated long separations but the "buddies" weathered the physical and emotional distances. We were not surprised when they announced their engagement soon after graduation and plans for a December wedding moved immediately into high gear.

*   *   *

Heidi is an attractive, self-confident young woman, extremely intelligent and capable, but the weariness of the last fifteen hours showed. The raw vulnerability of a new widow made her look much more like a little girl than a twenty nine year old woman. Yet again, we all seemed caught up in an unrealistic swirl of clashing emotions, the kind of turmoil that turns tongues to stone. Everyone begins grasping for words that they know will only sound stupid but must be said anyway. I thought that Heidi's beautiful face was showing the signs of shock gradually being replaced by an unbelieving pain.

The conversation of that morning, had it been recorded, would probably be described as comforting by anyone hearing it but my recollection of it is just the opposite. Of necessity, much of it was taken up with the "arrangements" and the rest with each of us in turn trying desperately to put down the rising anger at the unfairness of it all. I recall being comforted only by being in the presence of the woman that Gary loved so dearly. If his consciousness remained in any form, I knew he would be there with us that morning.

The most poignant moment, imbedded among the many unbearable ones that morning, came as Barbara found the strength to share with Heidi a few things that Gary had said during his visit with us. I'm not certain how she did it but she rose to the occasion beautifully. During their round of golf on Wednesday morning, he had mentioned that he was missing Heidi more than ever on this particular trip. Obviously, his career in the army had taken him away from home for extended periods of time in the past but this time, he said that he didn't know how he was going to bear the lengthy separation until he saw her again.

*   *   *

Gary was a soldier. Being away from home was part of the job and he accepted it. Heidi also knew what it meant to be a soldier's wife. She had observed what it meant in her brother's life and was well aware of the hardships that the life in the service could place on a marriage. She always handled the separations with her typical grace and style, without complaint.

Barbara and I were visiting Colorado Springs when Saddam Hussein ordered the invasion of Kuwait. We were scheduled to go to Fort Lewis in Seattle to visit with Pam and Gary joined us for a few days. On the second day, while we all were attending a Mariners-Red Sox game in Seattle, Gary called in to his unit at Fort Carson and returned to us with the news that he had to return to base. His unit was being deployed, he told us, and my stomach fluttered with that unique feeling of dread, nervousness and excitement combined. My relief matched his deep disappointment when he continued to explain that his deployment was to help fight forest fires in Oregon, not to fight Iraqis in Kuwait. It was only the third inning of the game and we left immediately. He was on a flight back that very night. Our son truly was a soldier, I decided, as if I had any doubt.

Disappointment at not going to Kuwait was one thing, but leaving a Red Sox game in the third inning! That really showed me something.

*   *   *

The decisions that have to be made so quickly in situations such as this are ludicrous. How can families and a young wife be expected to decide upon burial plans, upon caskets, upon services, upon anything under those conditions? Much of Heidi's concern centered on Pam and her compassion for the incredible difficulties of proceeding with the wedding plans as we also "arranged" the funeral for her brother. We've always respected and admired Heidi but her ability to handle these difficult decisions was nothing short of amazing.

*   *   *

Heidi's recollections of the fourteenth of May, 1992:
   "The strongest memory I have is the profound look of grief and sadness in your faces as you walked in the door. . .the dark grayness of your expressions and the way our eyes met. . .the way that look made the whole horrible thing finally seem possible or real. It was like a punch in the chest or someone sucking all the breath out of me, and I remember wanting to flee to avoid it. And yet, at the same time, I felt a relief to finally be with both of you, people who really loved Gary and were feeling the same incredible shock and grief of it all. . .not that my family didn't love Gary and were devastated but it was different to be with the two of you, you know?"

*   *   *

"What would Gary want?" That question focused much of our discussion about the funeral arrangements. (Why is it always funeral arrangements and wedding plans? Why not funeral plans and wedding arrangements?) I've tried to imagine the conversations with him if he were alive but without success.

"What do you think, Gary? Should we go ahead with the wedding or what?"

"Where would you like to be buried, Gar?"

"What kind of casket would you prefer?"

The necessity of making these decisions forces us to think that way but I'm afraid that sometimes it seems rather presumptuous. I remember thinking how arrogant Pete Rozelle, Commissioner of the National Football League, was when he explained his decision to allow the teams to play on the Sunday following the assassination of John Fitzgerald Kennedy. The President certainly would have wanted us to play, he assured us, as though he had a direct line to the hereafter.

When we finally have nothing more to fall back on, nothing more to help us, we use that reasoning. We all were certain that Gary would have wanted the wedding to go on as planned. He loved our little town of Tuftonboro so he certainly would have wanted to be buried there.

Before leaving the house, we agreed to go to Mayhew's Funeral Home in Moultonboro on Saturday morning and assist Heidi with the selection of the casket and filling out the papers for the obituaries and death notices. Then, after another round of tearful hugs followed by sad good-byes, we headed for the next in the series of outrageous experiences human beings are required to go through while making the final "arrangements."

* * *

Tuftonboro is a small town filled with people who rally to support their neighbors in times of need or tragedy. It is also the typical New England town where bad news travels much faster than good. Russ Petrie had alerted Mary Craigue, the town clerk at the time, that we would be coming to purchase a burial site in the town cemetery. There was considerable activity in the town offices that Friday morning and as we entered the building, Mary immediately rose and greeted us. It is not my imagination that I sensed a respectful silence fall over the others as we followed her through the swinging gate and into the small office at the rear of the building.

Before filling out the necessary forms, Mary produced a grid, a layout of the cemetery, and pointed out exactly where the site would be. Barbara and I had decided long before that we would be cremated; it seemed the proper and unselfish thing to do at the time. After all, space is at a premium and we all know that "dust to dust, ashes to ashes" is a truism. Our opinion changed abruptly when we realized that our son would be buried in the town cemetery. Our altruistic motives vanished in the harsh light of reality and we purchased two additional plots so that we would be spending eternity near our son. Looking at the plot plan reminded us of choosing a house lot in a large subdivision. We picked the plots and filled out the required forms.

The Tuftonboro Town House cemetery spreads out behind the town offices on familiar ground for me. As we walked out to find the plot, memories of past bow hunting expeditions flooded over me. The wooded section between the cemetery and Spider Web Gardens was a favorite place to enter the prime hunting territory behind the expansive nursery and I often parked my car on the edge of the cemetery before entering the woods. Gary had gone with me on several occasions, although I always knew his heart wasn't into killing anything.

"Gary would really like this," I remember saying, again speaking for him in his permanent absence and regretting it instantly.

.

* * *

"Don't come down from the tree until I come to get you," I said with the authority of an experienced hunter but I'm sure it sounded more like a father admonishing his son in advance. It was late one crisp autumn afternoon when I settled Gary with his bow into a tree stand on a well-worn deer trail. There was at least a decent chance that he might see a deer, if even from a distance.

"I won't be back until dusk so don't get antsy. If you hit something, wait an hour then start hollering and I'll hear you. Other-

wise, just stay put." I continued into the forest and found a second stand far enough away from his to not interfere but close enough to hear his shouting.

Over two hours later, as darkness began to overtake the forest, I climbed down, disappointed that neither of us had any luck. As I walked slowly back up the trail toward Gary's stand, I decided I wouldn't call out. Instead, I'd just test his patience a little.

I'm sure that the crunching sound of my footfalls on the leaves was reaching him and I wondered how he was reacting. In the forest, darkness comes fast after the sun sets and I was within fifty yards of his stand when I heard his shaky voice.

"Dad," he said. "Dad, is that you?" I stopped, enjoying the impromptu game of hide and seek. "Dad?" he asked, his voice quavering even more. I took a few steps closer before calling to him.

"Were you scared?" I asked when I arrived at the bottom of his tree. I thought I knew what his answer would be but he surprised me.

"Yeah, I was," he said, "but I saw three deer earlier." After he climbed down, he explained why the logistics of the shot prevented him from even drawing his bow. I knew he couldn't shoot at them and I understood completely. We didn't hunt together again after that.

*   *   *

Visits from our New Jersey relatives and friends highlighted the twenty-two years we had lived in New Hampshire. At the beginning, showing off the beautiful countryside with its pristine lakes and towering mountains competed with the simple pleasure of seeing people who played important roles in our lives. After several visits, the novelty of our New Hampshire existence gradually diminished and we anticipated the visits more for the simple joy of maintaining the New Jersey connections. Pam's wedding promised to be a New Jersey reunion of monumental proportions with dozens of family and friends in attendance.

The experience at the cemetery, painful beyond measure, was behind us and for the remainder of the day we could look forward to a succession of equally painful reunions with guests who now were arriving for both a wedding and a funeral. The excitement of seeing our close friends and relatives created as ambivalent a feeling as I have ever experienced. I knew my Aunt Elaine and Uncle Dan would be the first. They and their friends, the Rileys, always left New Jersey at such an early hour on their trips to New Hampshire that I was sure they would be at our house by early afternoon. I recall that as we drove home from the cemetery, I was visualizing the meeting with them. I wondered whether God would supply the emotional strength we would all need when we saw them.

*   *   *

The Army-Navy football game is unique in the world of sports. The spectacle and pageantry combines with the innocent flamboyance of cadets and midshipmen to create an atmosphere unmatched, even by the most prestigious college football powers across the country. The generosity of Elaine and Dan Punch made our attendance at the first one of Gary's cadet career so memorable that it remains the kind of experience that is mentioned any time we are together.

The small ranch house in Stratford, New Jersey, has been their home for over forty years. When Gary began talking about the Army/Navy game, Elaine and Dan announced that their house would serve as the "base of operations" for the weekend. Elaine's twin, my Aunt Elly, lived in an apartment directly across the street and she offered any available space for overflow. The result was that both places were filled to overflowing with cadets bunking on sleeping bags on the floor in virtually every room and Elaine serving huge breakfasts and a dinner of dozens of rolls spilling over with "barbecue," a special sloppy joe recipe of my grandmother's. The entire weekend was unforgettable and was repeated many times through the West Point careers of Gary and Pam. The spe-

cial bonds created during these special, laugh-filled experiences made Elaine and Elly very special to the cadets in our family.

*   *   *

About one-thirty that afternoon, I heard the Riley's van turn into our driveway. Vince Riley, one of the funniest people I have ever known, usually arrived at our house with the horn blaring and shouting through the open window. That day, even Vince was subdued. It was time for me to dismantle another barrier as I watched them approach. I greeted them wordlessly because I honestly couldn't speak. My Aunt Elaine is seldom speechless; her ability to converse without stopping for a breath is legendary. That day, she, too, was silent as she hugged me. For a time, we all just stood there, seemingly frozen to the spot as though we were on the verge of cracking and any movement would shatter us. The ambivalence returned like the scales of justice that teeter back and forth. On one side is the enfolding warmth of love that people who are dear to us always bring with them. Just as that side begins to take control, the cognizance of the pain about to be shared sends the balance skittering in the other direction. How can one want so badly to see another person yet dread it at the same time? I thought of how much I wanted to see our special friends, the Gares and the Caldwells, yet shuddered at the prospect of their scheduled arrival later that evening. It was just twenty-four hours since I received Jeri's phone call at Kennett. It seemed as though it could have been a minute or a lifetime.

*   *   *

Unexpectedly, the rehearsal for the wedding provided a respite. The presence of Russ Petrie and his ability to be in charge of a situation when necessary lent a sense of sanity to the proceedings. There actually were moments when the activity was sufficiently intense to move to the forefront despite the crushing grief that was superimposed over everything. Russ's assurances that he would make a short statement at the beginning of the wedding service put

us at ease. We knew he could handle the situation as well as anyone. There was, however, no possibility that Barbara and I could
attend the rehearsal dinner. Pam understood and urged us to do
whatever would be most comfortable. At that time, the thought of
watching the rest of the world going on with their lives, which it
inevitably would, was not an option for us. After the rehearsal, we
simply went home and waited for the next first time visitors and
the inevitability of balancing the scales of happiness and grief.

*   *   *

*The Punches and the Rileys along with Pam and a few others sat
on the porch having cocktails after the wedding rehearsal. With
the rehearsal dinner scheduled for seven that evening, Pam had
time to visit with us before getting ready. The conversation lacked
the liveliness that always followed whenever Elaine or Vince
were present and especially with the two of them in the same
room. One never knew in that situation what harmless word or
phrase or comment might trigger a memory that would then rain
down a cascade of helpless emotion so for the most part the conversation remained innocuous.*

*At some point, a loud crash came from the living room. We all
heard it and looked at each other. I went to investigate. What I
found was temporarily meaningless. When I returned and shared
it with others, it proceeded quickly through the gamut of accident
to coincidence to a sign similar to finding the golf ball in the
road.*

*A framed photograph of Pam, Jeri and Gary taken at Jeri's
wedding had fallen from the bookcase in the living room. The
glass did not break. Of course, we came up with numerous reasons for it to have fallen- a door slamming, a careless dusting
that left it too close to the edge of the shelf, a defective stand on
the frame. Everyone nodded in agreement; it must have been one
of those explanations. As nearly as I can recall, that picture had
resided on that shelf for months. When I replaced it after our
discussion, I experienced the same unsettling sensation I felt*

when finding the golf ball. The timing of the fall of that photograph was impeccable and it certainly caught our attention.

* * *

"I have only slipped away into the next room. I am I and you are you.

Whatever we were to each other, that we still are. . .

Why should I be out of mind because I am out of sight? I am waiting for you, for a while, somewhere very near, just around the corner. . . and all is well."

Canon Henry Scott Holland, 1847-1918

Just around the corner, slipped into the next room . . .Just another of those coincidences!

* * *

Gary's stuffed shells found some takers and our guests were able to eat them for dinner that evening. Barbara and I found some other options among the many choices we had prepared for what we thought would be a whole week of celebration. The Punches and Rileys returned to their hotel at about nine o'clock. The rehearsal dinner wouldn't be over for at least another hour and we were left with a deafening quiet in the house. As we waited for the Gares and Caldwells, my discordant emotions returned with a vengeance.

* * *

Lifetime friends like the Gares are blessings in our lives. I'm not sure that we ever really appreciate them enough. They are the kind of people who thrive on doing good for others. No favor, no matter how complicated, and no request, no matter how bizarre, is ever refused.

Gary's "buddy" was spending most of her junior year in college in Germany on an exchange program and he managed to hitch a ride on an Air Force transport out of Maguire Air Force Base in New Jersey to see her during spring break. When he re-

turned to Fort Dix by the same method, he was broke. The phrase that was popular with cadets for the situation was to be without sufficient cash flow. It was late in the evening and his leave from West Point didn't end until late the next day.

Fort Dix is over an hour away from the Gares' home in Edge-water Park and the night he arrived, a torrential rainstorm was in progress. As is the case with most adult children, Gary in a crisis automatically would call his parents to help him. A single phone call to the Gares and Jerry was on his way to get him at Fort Dix. After bringing him back to their home, they marveled at his appe-tite as he devoured a large cookie sheet filled with Irene's home-made loaded pizza followed by an enormous bowl of spaghetti and meatballs.

"It's hard to live on love," he joked as he described the diet of bread and wine that he and Heidi subsisted on for virtually the en-tire visit in Germany.

The next day Jerry made certain that he had money in his pock-et and arranged a ride for him back to West Point, making sure that he had all of the resources he needed..

On another occasion, Cadet Gary called his mother at work to complain that Trailways Bus Company wouldn't accept a check for the fare from Washington to West Point and he had no cash. She happened at the moment to be quite busy and suggested, rather strongly I suspect, that he call me at work instead. I naturally did what parents have always done. I bailed him out, providing my credit card number to the cashier so the ticket could be charged to our account. The fact that we were over five hundred miles away had no bearing; parents solve crises for their children; that's what they do. He endured much good-natured teasing and many laughs at his expense over that incident, especially from the Gares.

Gary's death was especially painful for our wonderful friends. They had been with us through the inescapable roller coaster ride that is the raising of any child. They laughed with us as we tried every parenting psychology trend to counter the sibling rivalry be-tween Gary and his sisters. They shared our pride and joy as they watched him maneuver through the difficult adolescent years and finally grow into an exceptional young man.

* * *

The clashing anticipation of their arrival exceeded expectations. We rushed to meet them in our front yard, arriving at the car simultaneously as they climbed out. Over the years, Barbara has endured much teasing for her exuberant greetings, especially her "It's SO GOOD to see you!" This time there was no enthusiastic greeting and no teasing. The only words I recall being spoken as we all moved toward the front door in group hug fashion was a mumbled comment from Bud Caldwell.

"Pretty tough," he said. I couldn't even respond.

Not long after they arrived, Jeri and Pam came home, early departures from the partying after the rehearsal dinner. I felt that the closeness of the sisters never was more important. I was happy that they had each other and that Jeri's husband Duane had agreed to handle the responsibilities of the children so they could be together. When the girls arrived home to say that the post dinner party was still going strong, I experienced one of those times when I felt angry that the world was not stopping. There were people still having a good time out there as we wrestled with a penetrating sorrow. I would admit here to something that must be taken within the context of the situation. This was the first of several times during the week when I wondered if Gary's death could subconsciously be considered an intrusion by people who had never known him yet were being affected by him. This is a difficult concept at best but I do recall thinking about the fact that our son had died yet the parties rolled on. What a strange and cruel joke to be visited upon my fun-loving daughters who, of all people, should have been enjoying the evening!

Had circumstances been normal, this would have been a night of reminiscences, surrounded as we were by old friends and the remaining members of the Southard family but the memories that may have been shared instead stayed locked away in the minds of everyone there. That night would be the first one in our long friendships that didn't include an endless supply of hearty laughs. Bud told none of his hilarious stories, tales told in classic pantomime worthy of Charlie Chaplin. Jerry refrained from sharing the usual spate of new jokes he always had in copious supply. It certainly ranked as one of the strangest nights I've ever experienced. Any attempt at conversation began in whispered tones and faltered quickly. It was as though the angel of death had passed through and struck us all dumb. Mostly, we just sat in stunned silence.

Chapter Seven
Hell- Saturday
The Wedding Day
May 16, 1992

Anyone who has experienced a death in the family knows that sleep is a luxury for those in mourning. I had the persistent feeling that if I could just sleep through the night without awakening, the horrid bad dreams would be vanquished by the breaking light of a new day. I estimate that about thirty seconds elapsed between the initial coming into a conscious state and the crushing realities of what the birth of this new day would bring. With each passing second of awareness, the sadness grew in exponential fashion until the rest of the day began to play out in my mind.

First, in the morning, we would join Heidi for the inconceivable task of choosing a casket for our son. I recall wondering how on earth does one do that? What frame of reference does a parent use in helping to make that decision? Then, at six that evening, our daughter would be getting married. The ceremony, the reception, the rituals, the dancing, and everything else associated with weddings would go on. The adage that indeed "life does go on" would be proven once again. The bizarreness of the day ahead could easily qualify it for a sick, black comic skit on one of Gary's favorite television programs, *Saturday Night Live*.

*   *   *

Gary and Heidi, close buddies that they were in high school, enjoyed watching Saturday Night Live together. When he used it as a reason to dodge our "home by midnight" rule, he never knew that one of the reasons we agreed to his request to stay at Heidi's until it was over was that we also had used the same ploy while in high school. The only difference was that our excuse was the original late night show starring Steve Allen. We did like the show but for a high school couple who were "going steady," the program was

secondary to the few precious extra minutes it allowed us to spend
together. There are some things that parents really do understand
in spite of their children's doubt that they could ever have felt the
same way.

*   *   *

Dread is too tame a word to describe how I felt as we traveled with
Heidi to the funeral home. When my mother passed away, I accompanied my father to assist in selecting the casket. I was a
young man then, only twenty-four, and with no experience with the
death of anyone close to me. I remembered that we were escorted
into a showroom filled with various models. All the options were
explained in great detail, from different wood finishes and patterns
to varying degrees of padding and pillows to solid brass or stain-
less steel hardware. The thought of experiencing the whole process
again was overwhelming. But this was, after all, our only son and I
needed desperately to see where he would be, as if it really made
any difference to him. The interesting discovery I made was that
there are remarkable similarities in death and in life. Through it all,
beginning to end, parents want the best for their children. I knew it
would take a tremendous act of will not to gravitate toward the
most expensive model with the best options, as though we were
buying him his first car.

The funeral director, a friend of Heidi's family, performed his
professional duties admirably, giving sound advice and counsel as
we walked solemnly among the displays. I am sure that had I been
asked to describe the coffin the day after the funeral, I could not
have done it. Unlike births and graduations and weddings and re-
tirement parties, funerals are not photographed and the highlights
are not forever etched in memory. I believe that we want to forget
everything about them as quickly as possible. I've never had anyone ask if I would like to see a family album of funeral pictures.
Much of our human resiliency to tragedy hinges on our ability to
forget. As important as my son's casket was to me at that time, I
wanted to forget it as soon as possible.

The dread of the process diminished somewhat after we made the selection. The director took us into his office and we began the paper work that had to be completed. With the assistance of George Hluk, Gary's roommate and best friend at West Point, his obituary was written. It was George who understood the perplexing terminology used in the United States Army and he provided the information for the many schools Gary had attended and the service awards he had earned. What a strange experience it is to listen to a funeral director ask the questions necessary to fill in the details of a young man's life for a two or three paragraph obituary. It has the distinct feel of a cereal box contest that allows the contestants twenty-five words or less to explain their opinions on subjects better suited for a lengthy expository essay.

* * *

From the Granite State News, *May 20, 1992: This covers Gary's thirty years on the planet, less two months, obituary fashion.*

Voted "most likely to succeed" by his Kingswood Regional High School classmates, Southard quickly filled that role in his professional career. He was a four-year varsity athlete at Kingswood, excelling on the ski, cross-country and track teams. He was also an honor student and took part in numerous musicals and dramatic productions. Following graduation in 1980, he entered the United State Military Academy at West Point, where he joined the glee club and captained the (Nordic) ski team.

Southard graduated from West Point in 1984 and advanced through several military schools, including the U.S. Army Ranger and Airborne schools. Among numerous service medals he earned were the Army Service Medal, the Army Occupation Medal, the Army Commendation Medal (1 Oakleaf Cluster), the Humanitarian Service Medal, the Ranger Tab, the Airborne Badge and the Expert Infantryman's Badge. Most recently, the commander of Alpha

Company 2nd of the 12th Infantry (4th Division Mechanized), Southard had also served in the Army's elite Berlin Brigade and won an appointment for advanced civil (engineering) schooling at the Colorado School of Mines.

A resident of Tuftonboro most of his life, Southard and his wife, Heidi Gruner Southard, a Kingswood classmate and daughter of Moultonboro Town Clerk, Marguerite Gruner, lived in Colorado Springs, Colorado, for the past 3 ½ years.

Marshall Hewitt, another Kingswood graduate, wrote the article for the local weekly newspaper. The obituaries and death notices that appeared in other newspapers were much briefer.

Unlike the West Point sword that has been a center piece of our living room wall since he presented it to us at Christmas of his senior (Firstie) year, these articles and notices remain in a box filled with cards and letters of sympathy from that awful time. I know the power that resides in that box from painful experience as I continue to refer to it for this book. The passage of time is unable to dim the grief that wells up from that box every time I open it.

Inevitably, from among the hundreds of notes it contains, I'll see a name on an envelope or recognize the handwriting of a particular person and that is enough to transport me back. As one might guess, I make my trips to that box only under the duress of necessity. It is not filled with light reading for passing the time on a lazy Sunday afternoon.

*   *   *

My only request for the visiting hours on Sunday night was that the casket remained closed. From all the readings I had done in preparation for teaching my "Dead Is A Four Letter Word" class, I knew the purpose of the funeral process well. Closure was the key word that kept emerging. We must have closure before we can move on, the experts tell us. Viewing a dead body often supplied that sense of closure, I remember reading, but I did not want any part of being in the same room with my son's body in full view as I met the constant stream of friends and acquaintances sure to be there on Sunday evening. A favorite eight by ten photograph of him in his full dress uniform from West Point would provide enough closure for me and I was sure for others as well. A closed casket it would be.

The coffin and its options chosen, the obituary written and the services planned, we finally left the director's office and escaped into the sunshine of late morning on a warm May day. It was just over five hours to the wedding.

* * *

Heidi reminisces about those days:

"I remember not wanting to be indoors. I felt claustrophobic and trapped inside. I didn't want to see the cards, the flowers, the food, the people who were there who wouldn't be there unless something bad had happened. I wanted to be outside where there was room to breathe and space. . .and peace."

* * *

Before we left the funeral parlor (Isn't parlor such a soft word for such a harsh place?) we agreed to accompany Heidi and her brother to visit with Gary, laid out, euphemistically speaking, in an open casket on Sunday morning. It was a quiet ride back to Marguerite's house, as though finalizing the "arrangements" had collected all of our energies and then beaten them into submission. Then it was home to prepare for the wedding. On the afternoon horizon, I could see the lineup of untold numbers of those human barriers we were sure to encounter for the first time at the ceremony.

* * *

"There is a whole town out there waiting to help," said a former professional colleague of mine who lives in our lovely little town of Tuftonboro. "All you need do is ask," she added.

Just as most people have difficulty with phrase selection when greeting someone after a death, the one greeted usually has an equally difficult time having an answer for that most frequent of offers.

"If there is anything I can do, just let me know" or some other similar expression is so common, so sincere and so compassionate that it begs for a positive response. Most often, unfortunately, there is not an appropriate response or at the very least, no answer that makes sense.

The house bustled with the excitement of the wedding day when we returned, an excitement dulled by brutal realities. We found that many people answered the unanswerable "What can I do?" question themselves by supplying ample supplies of food of every description. Casseroles, breads, cookies, and fruit baskets filled the dining room table. Our friends and relatives had stopped by to check on us and were busy assisting with the organization of the food. Not surprisingly, Irene Gares and Diane Tepe, both extremely competent and experienced with handling crowds of people for meals, assumed a joint leadership role, efficiently turning their abundant positive energy toward creating order from potential chaos. Soon after we arrived, the visitors began to drift back to their motels and homes to get dressed for the wedding.

Barbara and I agreed that it would be best if we arrived at Perry Hollow Golf and Country Club well before even the earliest of the guests. There were to be many visitors from a distance away and we knew it would be best if we saw them before the wedding rather than seeing them for the first time as they went through the receiving line. We were thankful for the help and priceless support from our family and friends and equally as thankful to have a chance to get off the emotional roller coaster of the morning before climbing aboard another later that afternoon.

*   *   *

A daunting barrier to my emotional stability that afternoon was my first meeting with Sister Grace Jones, likely the only person I have ever met who fit into my category of saints on earth. A Lutheran deaconess and life long friend of Barbara's mother, she had founded the Kensington Dispensary, a facility for brain-damaged children. By the time of Pam's wedding, Sr. Grace was severely disabled and we truly doubted that she would be able to make the trip from her home in Pennsylvania. She explained to us that her close relationship with Pam precluded any possibility that she wasn't going to attend this wedding. As avid a game player as Nan, Sister Grace always joined in the regular games of rummy and other card games with Pam and as "adjunct game player" developed a special relationship with her. Gary's death and her best friend's pain made it certain. It was Pam's wedding and Nan needed her. She wasn't going to miss it.

With the help of another friend, Laura Fultz, they made the long trip by car. The club was not handicapped accessible. I left the logistics of seeing that Sister Grace, wheelchair bound and somewhat overweight because a long struggle with diabetes and heart problems, made it to the second level of the sprawling clubhouse with Jerry Gares and Bud Caldwell. Happy to be given a job to do, ("If there is anything I can do, let me know!") they also arrived at the club early to assist in any way they could.

I stood on the second floor balcony and saw Laura's car stop at the entrance. By the time I walked down the stairs, Laura already had Sister Grace out of the car and sitting in her wheel chair, ready for what looked to be an exciting trip being carried up two flights of stairs. As I reached her chair and looked down at her, she took both of my hands, her eyes filling. I always thought she had the kindest, softest eyes I'd ever seen and I enjoyed teasing her and making them sparkle. I remember distinctly that she didn't say a word. She just looked at me and squeezed my hands.

Sister Grace Jones always seemed to me to be operating on a higher plane than we other humans that surrounded her, as if she knew something that the rest of us were desperately trying to figure out. Never was that feeling stronger than that day. There was no sparkle in her eyes but there was understanding and that was all I needed from her. I think she knew that.

Then, the interesting trip up the steps began, amidst much smiling and lighthearted joking. Little more than a month later, Sister Grace died during open-heart surgery. Her last words to her friend, Laura Fultz, captured her faith, her dignity and her sense of humor all at once.

"If I don't wake up here," she said, "I'll see you over there."

I like to think that Gary was there to meet her.

*   *   *

A wise decision, Barbara and I agreed, as the guests began arriving and we faced them, one emotional meeting after another. I believe that as powerful as each of those first meetings were, a mutual strength was shared. Despite my firm belief that first meetings are difficult, I recognize that they serve a purpose for both parties and we were grateful for every piece of positive energy we could absorb from those connections. As difficult as they were, the feeling remained the same throughout the entire weekend and beyond.

We encouraged the guests to take advantage of the beautiful views from the balcony surrounding the entire second story of the club as we waited for the bride to arrive in the limousine. With the wedding scheduled for a six o'clock start, we circulated among the guests until about five forty-five and then drifted toward our assigned places with a hug and a silent squeeze of the hands. There really wasn't much that could be said. I found my way to the lower level and stood in the driveway, looking out at the White Mountains in the distance.

Perry Hollow sits perched near the top of Copple Crown Mountain. Any attempt at an adequate description of the view is futile. To the west, just under the setting sun, Lake Winnipesaukee spread out like a giant amoeba while the still snow covered Mount Washington glistened to the north. It is the kind of view that doubles and triples property values and makes tourists from the "flatlands" gasp in awe and appreciation.

To ignore the beauty of it is criminal yet I know that as I stood alone waiting for Pam and her entourage to arrive, I did just that. I believe that was one of the few brief periods of time since Gary's death that I had actually been alone and aloneness usually brings a sort of peace, especially in that setting. It didn't happen; I paced back and forth like an expectant father. I wanted this wedding to be perfect for Pam; nothing else was acceptable to offset her terrible predicament. During those moments, I felt as much anger toward whatever controls our destiny in this life as I've ever endured. In philosophical hindsight and self-psychoanalysis, perhaps it was the magnificence of the surroundings clashing so sharply with the injustice of my son's death and my daughter's pain that was the source. Who knows?

My pacing was interrupted by the sound of a car approaching on the long driveway. I was sure it was the limousine. Pam and company were on the verge of being late. Instead the car turned into the parking lot and Norie and Frank Wisniewski got out. I saw yet another first time barrier unexpectedly looming in front of me. I was shaking as I strode out to meet them and crumbled as Norie hugged me. I'm certain that after I recovered, I said something innocuous, probably about the weather or the view, as we walked toward back toward the clubhouse. I hope they drew at least a portion of the shared strength they brought with them.

Frank and I have been friends since high school. I was best man at their wedding and yet there was nothing in our collective memory to prepare us to meet in this particular circumstance. It is amazing how awkward a death can make us, even in the presence of our closest family and friends. They entered the clubhouse and I renewed my pacing, waiting for my now fashionably late daughter to arrive as the sun began its striking descent toward the horizon.

*   *   *

Frank sent a letter to us shortly after he returned from the wedding, expressing his disappointment at not be able to stay for the Sunday and Monday "arrangements" and rituals scheduled to follow as our attention turned from our daughter's wedding to our son's funeral. His perceptive observations are worthy of note as the Wisniewski visits to Tuftonboro and our small church were rare.

"The support system that was evident from your friends and church in New Hampshire must have helped you considerably," he wrote. "I think it is wonderful that you are so strong in your faith in God. One of the blessings is that while knowing the 'Whys' of life is always helpful, when there is no 'why' and maybe never will be, your faith can carry you past the unexplained."

I believe that my old friend must have sensed my anger that evening when they arrived, an anger and questioning that my faith was having a very difficult time overcoming.

"You and we are all blessed with such wonderful memories of Gary," he continued. "He was such a marvelous individual with so many achievements reflecting his strong will. . . Your loss is great but so must be your pride in your son."

On that spectacular evening, surrounded as I was by family, friends and the extraordinary natural beauty of Copple Crown Mountain, I struggled with the breathtaking knowledge that memories are not enough. Much too soon, they become ethereal, gradually turning to misty visions of a past that sometimes seems never to have been real.

I agree with the sentiment expressed in one of the cards residing in our own Pandora's Box of emotions---"Memories are like stars in the dark night of sorrow." There are occasions when a heavy overcast prevents us from enjoying those stars. I wondered if the sky would ever clear for me.

*   *   *

After a late beginning, the wedding proceeded in a timely fashion. As Russ Petrie had promised, he had spoken to the guests at the start. The theme of his comments was one that would become familiar as in succeeding years, he often preached on similar topics. Human lives, by their very nature, are blessed by joy and cursed by sadness and on this particular weekend, we just happened to be experiencing both in a microcosm of time and space. For any guest who may have been unaware, he touched briefly upon the unique circumstances surrounding this ceremony and the decision to go forward with the wedding.

Many of the letters and cards we received mentioned the courage and fortitude that our family exhibited as we went through the motions of wedding rituals and customs. While eternally grateful to all who shared their admiration, I feel a need to correct what I see as a serious misconception as far as my behavior is concerned. I am speaking here only for myself as the rest of our family deserves all the credit and more for their grace under fire. Ernest Hemingway would have been proud of them. Barbara and our two daughters were as radiant and vital as ever. I marvel when I look at the wedding album, searching for clues to the crushing pain I know they were feeling, only to find it masked by their poise and elegance. They, I've decided, are the brave people mentioned in so many of the cards.

*   *   *

A sampling of sentiments from the infamous box that harbors so much . . .

"We want to thank you for having the courage to show your love to Pam and Andy by making their wedding day perfect." Mary and Bob Lohman (Andy's parents)

"I admire the strength you and your family have to have carried on with and for your daughter during her wedding." Sig (a friend of Barbara's)

"The two of you and your family were so courageous and elegant through the ordeal of this weekend!" Bud Caldwell (a family friend)

*   *   *

The father of the bride was numb. There could be no doubt about summoning the strength required to get through the night but it was not about bravery; it was about paralysis. It was about going through the motions. It was about not even realizing that all you were doing was putting one foot in front of the other.

The photographs show a smiling but typically emotional dad walking his "baby" daughter toward the marriage altar and a father and daughter dancing the traditional "daddy's little girl" dance. What they don't show, what they can't show, is the undeniable fact that I may as well have been operating in a hypnotic trance.

There are many jokes about the role of the father of the bride at a wedding, most of them having to do with his giving away the bride then emptying his checkbook and pockets. If that had been the only role I had to play that night, how happy I would have been. All the components for a memorable wedding were present; the elegance, the grace, the customs, the socializing, the music, the ceremony, old friends and new, family, the setting. What was probably missing was a fully functioning father of the bride. There are images of that night that can be dredged from the bank of memories but unlike the seared in memories of the previous two days, they are fitful and incomplete. Only a few minutes of that long evening are clear; the rest of it remains a muddied collection of disjointed, incoherent reflections in the deep stream of consciousness that spans those hours.

We remember events or conversations because of their impact on us. The lighter the impact, the less likely the event will be remembered in all its nuances. My description of the wedding and reception will not be adequate for this reason. I'm concerned that the events will somehow be diminished by what follows. It may seem as though most of the evening was not important since I will write about only those memories that are clear and easily envisioned. This is not intended to lessen the impact of that event on others but to explain what was happening from my perspective. Please do not assume from my description that a somber shadow dampened the enthusiasm of the guests. Actually, in a strange way, the circumstances may have intensified the level of celebration. My innocent observation to Russ Petrie the day before might explain what I mean.

I mentioned to Russ that at least half of the guests at the wedding had never met Gary and that was a good thing. It would be much easier for them to put aside any gloom that might exist. A dramatic but not quite accurate analogy could be drawn from an Edgar Allen Poe short story that I taught for many years. While the plague lurked just outside the solid doors of the castle in "The Masque of the Red Death," the revelers inside attempted to ignore the pall its presence cast over them by engaging in increasingly frenetic celebration. Pam and Andy's wedding and reception obviously were not equal to that level of dramatics but for a few hours, it provided an escape from the reality that the next day would bring back with a vengeance.

*   *   *

A week after the wedding and less than a month before she died, Sister Grace wrote this note to us.

". . .I wish I could do more to help but I realize that my prayers for you are the best I can do. Pam's wedding was lovely and you did everything you could possibly do to make it a happy time for Pam and Andy. Thank you so much for including us. I was so thankful that I could be there. I am also very thankful that I could be with you and Marion, Heidi and the girls in your deep sorrow."

It's probably heretical in light of all of us being created in the image and likeness of God, but I've always believed that prayers from Sister Grace had more influence with Him who hopefully was listening. I was thankful for that note and for her prayers.

*   *   *

By Saturday evening, the small town web of invisible lines of communication had circulated the news of Gary's death. Wolfeboro and Tuftonboro are typical of small New Hampshire towns in many respects, including, as mentioned previously, being places where good news travels fast and bad news even faster. Our wedding guests were offered two options for over night stays and both proprietors knew the situation. Most of our family chose the Pine

View Motel in Melvin Village while the "younger" folks stayed in the more exciting Wolfeboro environment at the Lake Motel. It was at the Lake Motel where long time friends from our Beaver Hollow Campground days were given the news about Gary.

*   *   *

It is one of those photographs that becomes etched in the collective family memory bank alongside graduation and wedding pictures and other momentous events. The picture is taken on the front steps of the campground as the family gathers on June 30, 1980, to say goodbye to Gary. The next day is R-Day, his first day at West Point, and several campers who happened to be at Beaver Hollow that morning joined in what became an emotional farewell. While his sisters turn their backs to hide the surprising tears for their sibling nemesis's departure, Barbara gives him his last "Mom's hug" and Ollie sits at his master's feet, supposedly not under-standing but surely sensing that something important is happening. Off to one side, in a small knot of interested campers, most of whom have known Gary through his four years in high school, Jane Blye also is turning away. The photograph has many other notable characteristics, like Gary's long blond hair soon to sheared by a West Point barber and the rustic camp store back-ground. However, the emotion being shared by those in the picture provides it with the power needed to retain its place in my memory. Whenever I think of that photograph, I think of Jane's part in it.

Jane and Phill Blye became seasonal summer campers shortly after we met them. There was an instant rapport between us and that rapport quickly turned into a solid friendship. Gary was the first of any of the children of either family to be leaving home for college and Phill and Jane shared our anxiety and trepidation of sending a son to West Point.

Ironically, they would be the first of our families to truly lose a child, not to a promising college or military career but to a speed-ing car on a New Year's afternoon as he crossed the road to his house, just yards away. Unimaginable, isn't it, to hear the squeal of brakes and rush to the scene, only to find your son as the victim?

I knew Phill and Jane represented one of the most formidable first time barriers yet to be confronted. I've often thought that a perfect analogy for these first meetings could be found wading in the breakers at the New Jersey shore. Some of the waves are mild, barely splashing to the waist as they pass by while others are so powerful that they can knock an unsuspecting bather flat on his back. Our first meeting with them loomed like one of those powerful waves, only its timing unknown to us.

*   *   *

Jane and Phill did not come to the wedding. The campground assumed its place in the rear view mirror of our life. In the eleven years since we had owned it, our connections with most things about it were receding quickly. We maintained regular contact with the Blyes but not regular enough for them to make the rather restricted guest list for the wedding. A phone conversation with them several weeks before revealed that they would be in the area on this particular weekend for a meeting and we asked them to at least stop in at the reception and say hello.

That phone conversation and invitation did not appear on the blank screen that was my mind that night. I've wondered since on many occasions about our good friends' reaction when they stopped at the Lake Motel to ask directions to Perry Hollow and were given the news. Think about that! In the wildest fantasy, would anyone expect to hear that sort of news in that situation?

We had made many memories with them. I experienced my first and only river canoe trip with them. We had campfires and pizza parties and reciprocal weekend visits and theater trips, all those entertaining escapades that friends share. Now they knew that we shared something far beyond any comparison to those adventures.

I believe that their decision to come to the reception to see us after finding out about Gary was truly courageous. It is a tribute to them as compassionate human beings that they cared enough to subject themselves to what they must have known would be a traumatic reunion, one that could only bring about a revisiting of their still healing wounds. Just as we're all certain that we would behave heroically in times of crisis, charging into burning buildings or facing down an armed robber, it is easy to assume that I would have done the same. The truth is that I wonder about that. After my experiences with the distress of seeing people for the first time after Gary's death, I sometimes am afraid that I would have lacked the courage to stop at the reception. How much easier it would be to write a note or call, the pain diluted by time and space. To their credit, Jane and Phill were right there.

*   *   *

Sifting through the notes and cards in "THE BOX," I am surprised at the number of them that mention a similar experience. A visit to your local greeting card and gift shop quickly reveals that there seems to be a card for very occasion, even for this one.

"I understand what you're going through, because I've experienced the loss of someone very dear in my life, too" the front of the card from Laura, Jane and Phill's daughter, says. "Someday, the pain will ease and the memories will bring comfort. Soon you'll find yourself back in the stream of things. I know. . .I've been there too."

The sentiments are sincere and I know that we appreciated the thoughtfulness of all those who sent notes and cards with similar messages at the time. I realize now that the passage of some time is necessary to truly appreciate what the notes were saying. I didn't feel that I was member of that "I've been there" club until years had passed. In the muddled and befuddled state of incessant grief, it doesn't always help to know that someone else has felt the some way. Misery doesn't always love company, to refute an accepted cliché.

Subconsciously and somewhat guiltily, I'm afraid I might have been thinking something like this.

"Yes, I'm sure that it must have been difficult for you but that was then and this is now. That was your son/daughter/mother/father/ whatever and we're talking about my son here."

I don't like to admit it but I'm afraid that I may have had thoughts like that. Now that I've joined that club, I try to avoid the pitfall of saying that I understand. I can relate but I'm not sure that I can understand. While grief is universal, I believe that the reactions to it are as varied as the individuality and personality of every member of the human race.

"Someday, the pain will ease and the memories will bring comfort. . ." the card continues. The pain does ease just from the weight of life that inexorably is piled on top of it. The memories so far rarely bring comfort; more often, they bring sadness and anger that what might have been will never be.

*   *   *

There are dances that are required of the father of the bride at a wedding reception and I'm sure I danced those. At least, our copy of Pam's wedding album tells me that I did. I'm certain that I was not on the dance floor very often after that but during one slow dance with Barbara, I looked across the room just as the Blyes reached the second landing of the stairs. We stopped dancing immediately and made our way to them. As soon as we were close enough to have eye contact, I knew that they had somehow heard about Gary. The expressiveness of the human face is astounding. A professional actor can use his eyes to project a whole catalogue of emotions but the eyes of our friends focused on us with only one--- profound sadness. The energized environment of a wedding reception formed a surreal backdrop for the gloom draped over what might have been a happy reunion with long-time friends.

Poignant is an overused word but it is the best word to describe our conversation with Phill and Jane that evening. The commonality of our experiences moved us into a different realm, a zone of despair that couldn't be avoided. They dispensed much sound advice that evening as only those who have "been there, done that" can but I'm afraid most of it was lost in the milieu of music and laughter emanating from the reception.

Combine the external noise with the internal state of mind and it is easy to understand the fogging of our perception.

*   *   *

"To ask parents to celebrate a daughter's wedding, knowing that in a couple of days they will be burying a son, has to be an unbelievable reliance on their faith and support from close friends." This is a quote from a note from Jim and Debbie Hopkins that helps explain our state of mind.

*   *   *

Not many recollections of that night emerge from the haze. With some research and discussions with guests and the caterer and the DJ, I'm sure that I could recreate the scene but I feel as though that would be tampering with what I am trying so hard to replicate. We do go through the motions of life in many different situations. We can be like Billy Pilgrim in *Slaughterhouse Five* and let our minds take us away from unpleasant or even dangerous predicaments. We can daydream our way through a boring sermon and will ourselves to think of pleasant experiences as the dentist performs a root canal procedure. My subconscious relief mechanism for the evening of the wedding allowed only certain elements to survive and they are what need to be shared. They represent the reality of that night. Heidi expresses the feeling so well.

*   *   *

"I don't remember a lot from that morning (Friday) or any of the first days after Gary died. I remember more the desperate feel of it all rather than the events. I remember feeling a desperate inner plea to slow everything down . . .because it was too much to take in . . .a feeling of if only we could all just sit down and talk it through we could fix it."

The search for something sane, making some sense of order out of the chaos is a basic human need and when that need can't be met, we tend to improvise. When things seem hopeless, we are forced into taking another tack to salvage our sanity. My selective reminisces of the wedding night likely fit into this category. Heidi used a different approach.

"I can't really recall how long we visited or anything we spoke about," she says, describing the first time we saw her after Gary's death. "I assume we talked about the events leading up to his death, because I remember wanting desperately to get the story straight . . .the where, the when, the who was there, the who said/did what . . .how long before help arrived, when did he get to a hospital, did he suffer . . .like getting the facts straight would somehow make the whole thing make sense. (It) probably was part of that desperate need to get some control of the situation."

*   *   *

The request of several members of the wedding party to extend the reception for an extra hour provided a heavy dose of reality, probably more than I was ready to accept at the moment. There was, after all, a party going on, a celebration of my daughter's wedding. The young people at the reception, with the wonderful and enviable ability to live in the moment, were having a great time. The DJ was willing; the bartenders were willing; the manager of Perry Hollow was willing. With a negligible added expense, there was no obvious problem. It is a moment that I remember vividly, not because it was an earth-shattering request but because it meant that I would have to stay in the celebratory mode for sixty more minutes. I will admit to watching the clock as the evening wore on; the day had stretched into a very long one.

Adding an hour onto the reception was a natural inspiration, one that could not be denied. The party was going strong; the guests were having a wonderful time. It would be cruel to bring it to premature end just because a few of us were ready to have it end. Of course, the decision could only go one way. It would only be another sixty minutes spent with the increasingly blunt reality that Sunday waited on the shadowy horizon. I retreated into the psychological fog as the party continued, spending another hour watching the pleasant scenes filled with the joy of the young. I was beginning to feel quite old.

Chapter Eight
Hell
Sunday, May 17, 1992

For both of us, attending the Sunday worship service at Melvin Village Community Church is an ingrained habit. Everyone draws something different from attendance at church but we always agreed that the hour spent in church on Sunday morning helped to center us for the coming week. Under the pastorate of Russ Petrie, the services often contained an emotional element along with a thoughtful message for the upcoming week. After the wedding reception, we discussed going to church the next morning. The people of our church have a well-earned reputation for protecting those in need or suffering. There we would be, enfolded by the love of people whom we loved, in a haven that we loved and, on this particular Sunday, joined by many of the visiting family and friends in town for the wedding, and now, of course, the funeral. It only made sense that we would go to church.

Impossible, we decided. Whether our decision was cowardly or simply being intelligent and realistic, or somewhere in between, the thought of placing ourselves into that emotional cauldron overwhelmed us. There would be no church for us on that particular Sunday.

*   *   *

Sometime Sunday morning, Barbara called to me from the living room. When I joined her, she pointed out a tiny red bud on the Christmas cactus plant that graced the shelf under our bay window. I was not exactly sure of how I should react since I know nothing about flowers and our houseplants were entirely her responsibility. My role, as I saw it, was to admire them when they produced beautiful blooms and to sympathize when they came to an unfortunate end.

What even I could notice was the singularity of the blossom. I remembered other times when the cactus would burst forth around Thanksgiving with dozens of blossoms and bloom continuously through the Christmas season. I had never seen a blossom in May. With each passing day, the blossom grew until it turned into a large, fully developed flower, its bright red petals opened wide.

"A rogue blossom" was my explanation, although I had no idea if there were such things.

Several weeks later, a sympathetic teacher at Kennett inquired about my mental state. At the time, he had a side business in hypnosis and his practice dealt mostly with helping people rid themselves of nasty habits like smoking and overeating and alcohol abuse. He also used regression therapy, an area of intense interest to me ever since reading The Search for Bridey Murphy when I was a sophomore in high school. Barbara also was a voracious reader of any books dealing with the subject of reincarnation and "the other side." I have since thought about being regressed on a number of occasions but each time have lost my nerve.

My answer to his inquiry was rather pat, the kind that takes on the cloak of cliché quickly.

"About as well as can be expected under the circumstances," I said, or at least something like that. For reasons that remain unclear to me even now, I followed my meaningless answer with a description of the Christmas cactus blossom that still held its full bloom status in our living room, although it was just beginning to droop.

I found his response fascinating and in retrospect, it could take on a life of its own if I let it. The exact phrasing is elusive but I know it was close to what follows. Regardless, the sense of it is as vivid and clear as it was that day.

"Oh," he said, "your son sent you a message." The short sentence was not hypothetical, not conjecture and not speculative. In his mind, he was making a simple statement of fact..

* * *

As expected, the Sunday worship service at the Melvin Village Community Church was attended by many of our wedding guests. Barbara's twin brother, Bob, was among them. He asked if we would mind picking him up at the church on our way to Mayhew's Funeral Home where Gary's body would be laid out for the family to visit. The day was another New Hampshire beauty, warm enough for some early boaters to be skimming across the lake, despite the still chilly water temperatures. The service ended just as we arrived and we parked well away from the church along the side of the road.

As we waited for Bob to come out, I'm guessing we probably slouched in our seats so as not to be noticed. The only member of our congregation who passed by was a friend who lived two houses from the church. She was clutching a handkerchief and dabbing her eyes. An insight flashed through my mind and I knew that her tears were for us. We did not attract her attention and she didn't notice us sitting in the car. It was like seeing an acquaintance two aisles over in the grocery store while on a hurried shopping trip. He really should be greeted but if he is, the quick shopping trip is extended and likely to become an inconvenience for everyone concerned. So, the easy way out is taken. The acquaintance becomes invisible and the meeting does not take place. Granted, this is a weak rationalization but a sound analogy. There are times when just greeting a friend seems that it might be more trouble than it is worth. I regret to say that this was one of those times.

The little white church sparkled against the backdrop of the pristine lake. Like the view from Perry Hollow atop Copple Crown Mountain the evening before, the setting contrasted harshly with our mission of that morning. Bob had seen the car and came over quickly.

Twenty-five minutes later, we were sitting in the parking lot of the funeral home waiting for Heidi and Elliot to arrive. I was beside myself with dreadful anticipation. Heidi had last seen Gary nine days before in Colorado Springs, his enthusiasm at its usual level when approaching a new school or training experience. Now, she would be seeing him for the last time, laid out in his Harry Connick, Jr. suit. I couldn't believe that she would have to go through this.

*   *   *

Pam and Andy's decision to be married in the traditional civilian wedding dress influenced Gary to bring along two of his civilian suits for the wedding. Early in the week, he allowed us to help him make his decision as to which one to wear, although we were sure that his decision had already been made. One of his suits looked just like one that his favorite performer, Harry Connick, Jr., might wear and there was little hope that our opinion would sway the decision if it differed from his. We decided that the "Connick suit" was by far the better choice and the next day, he took it to the local cleaners so that he would look as sharp as possible for his little sister's wedding. Heidi also liked Harry Connick and encouraged Gary to buy a suit of that style. I had been reminded of the discussion of the suit choice during our conversation with the Blyes the evening before. One of the bits of advice dispensed during that evening was Phill's adamant proclamation that anything may be buried with the deceased in the casket. I couldn't think of a single thing of Gary's that I could see any reason to send with him but there was no question which suit he would be wearing into eternity.

*   *   *

The entrance into the funeral home moved progressively down the scale from gloom into somber depression as the atmosphere slapped us in the face. The funeral director, as compassionate as any that I had ever met, escorted us into the lobby, asking as we went whether we wanted to go in together or separately. We hadn't discussed either possibility and looked at each other. A silent decision was made that we would enter the room together.

Throughout my career as an English teacher, my students probably tired of my harping on the ability of skillful writers to capture in words the full range of human emotion. This situation could have served as the ultimate challenge for the best of them. Imagine this. There are five people entering the "display" room. Two are the parents of the young man lying in the coffin. He was lifeless the last time they saw him on a hospital gurney four days before. A third is the young man's uncle. He has not seen his nephew for at least several years. The fourth is a brother-in-law, a comrade in arms, a fellow West Point graduate whose last memory of the man in the coffin is that of a vital and fit individual with whom he had much in common.

Now, picture this. The fifth is the young wife, a woman whose planned future was immutably intertwined with the "displayed" body just days before but now is left holding one end of the severed life line, shocked uncertainty and profound grief clouding her eyes.

The five of us inched into the room, tentative, on tiptoes, as though entering a darkened room in an amusement park fun house. The sight of Gary lying there confirmed my resistance to having an open casket for the visiting hours that evening. The strongest arguments for "closure" could not convince me that the best way to remember my son was standing by his open casket as lines of people filed past. Seeing him in this semi-private setting was all the closure that I could handle.

The room was large and the casket seemed to be centered in it. Ten or twelve straight-backed chairs were arranged in two rows facing him and I recall that we all immediately sat down, as though approaching the casket right away might represent a breach of etiquette. Over the course of the next hour, one by one, we moved toward the casket. Each of us held our own private conversations with him, just a soft murmur being heard by the others. Mine was a series of questions, like those I might have asked during one of our Sunday afternoon telephone conversations.

"How're you doing, Gar? Are things OK with you?" I know it sounds stupid but what else does a father do as he peers down at his son, a vulnerable little boy turned grown young man he just wants to shake to awaken from his sound sleep.

Unlike so many open casket displays I have seen, there is not a ready cliché that adequately described what I was seeing. He did not "look good" or "have good color." He was dead and unfortunately for all of us, he looked it. Periodically, the need to escape became overwhelming and I would leave for some fresh air. I approached his casket just once more after my first "conversation" with him. I was prepared to say goodbye or at least I thought I was.

The fresh air I had gulped in minutes before gave me the strength and momentarily cleared my head of the funeral parlor pall permeating my being. It also provided a chance to picture him as he lay there and I realized that there was one disturbing aspect of his appearance that bothered me. I went back in for my goodbye visit, determined to etch his face on my memory with such ferocity that it could never fade. My grandmother, the single most profound influence on my life when I was growing up, departed this earth in 1966 and I find it unsettling that I sometimes cannot resurrect her face. I couldn't let this happen with my son. When I moved close to him, I examined his closed eyes more closely. They betrayed the fact that he was dead, not just sleeping. I can still picture that face and the appearance of his eyes still disturbs me. The lids were sunken, as though there was nothing behind them, and I found that very disconcerting. The memory of his appearance before the lid closed forever is just a thought away and it is an appearance that always features the disquieting sunken eyelids.

* * *

The phenomenon is strange and I will never understand it. I've searched for a logical explanation and even for an explanation that would defy logic. Since there seems to be none, I'll simply present it with no explanation. You will have to supply your own.

The photo collage frame is cheaply made, its fake brass perimeter sprinkled with finger print smudges impossible to clean. There are spaces for nineteen pictures in it, ranging in size from 2x2 to 3X5. The photographs we selected for it capture four generations of our family. Obviously, Gary is in many of them, alone in only one. That one is a picture of him as a plebe racing in one of his first cross-country ski competitions for the Army Nordic Ski Team. The photograph that has caused me to mention this pictorial history of the Southard family resides in the upper right hand corner. Heidi, looking gorgeous, and Gary, looking dashing, are seated at an impeccably set table during a formal officers' dinner and dance in Berlin, Germany. It was taken shortly after Gary achieved the rank of captain and clearly shows the usual array of medals and awards that adorn the uniforms of most U. S. Army officers. He is a member of the Berlin Brigade in 1987, while Berlin was still a divided city. Gary had asked me to make a copy of this photograph from a slide that someone had given him. I remember transferring the picture into a snapshot format and making several copies, keeping one for us, the one that made it into the family collage.

For quite a while after Gary's death, I had studiously avoided the many pictures we had of him scattered about the house. Photographs, without exception, are taken to freeze in time moments that deserve to be relived or that should be preserved. As mentioned earlier, no one seems inclined to preserve in rich and vibrant color a picture of the cemetery plot as the casket is lowered into the ground. I had decided that the pictures of happy times filling our walls would have to wait until happier times to be enjoyed again.

About three weeks after Gary died, inspired by just a small splash of courage, I decided to look closely at some those "happy times" photographs. First, my eyes were drawn to a priceless picture of Gary and Heidi skiing somewhere in Colorado, most like-

ly their favorite resort of Breckenridge. I fought with the sadness of what might have been and moved my attention to the collage nearby, the largest of any frames that we had on the walls.

There was our family before Pam (difficult to imagine) and there were Nannie and Pop-Pop in New Jersey. My eyes caught Gary competing in the ski race and the smidgen of courage that had allowed me to begin to look at the photographs faltered. The collage has five pictures across the top and I forced myself to examine each one in order. The first one was Pam in her full dress parade uniform at West Point. An adorable picture of a young Jesse Mendenhall, our Godson, caused me to smile, just as it always had. A picture of Heidi as a senior in high school was next with Jeri and Duane's wedding photo filling the lower right hand corner just under a dazzling picture of Jeri as a high school junior. The photo of Heidi and Gary at the dinner is just above Jeri's picture. I looked closer and was transfixed by what I saw.

A small section toward the center of the photograph, not along the edge, had been removed. The piece is not more than a half an inch in length and only the surface is missing; the backing of the picture remains. The edges of the small piece are ragged, as though torn away. I know that I would have never used that photograph in the collage in that condition.

Several weeks later, I summoned enough courage, or perhaps curiosity, to take the collage apart. There was no trace of any missing piece that may have fallen behind the cardboard backing that holds all the photos in place. I truly wanted to find it but when I didn't, I simply put everything back the way it was, including the mysteriously damaged picture.

The piece that is missing contains his left eye. I'm not exactly sure when I finally shared this event with Barbara but I do know it was a long time. The bizarre nature of it made caused my hesitation; I had no idea how to explain it.

There is no explanation but I felt that it was time to share what to me is a baffling event. I sure that some day there will be a logical, physical explanation, similar to the rogue blossoms. Until then, please feel free to speculate. I have been doing just that for years.

* * *

When we arrived home from Mayhew's, our house was filled with our dear family and friends. They were people who had expected to be on their way home from an upbeat wedding weekend but instead were now waiting to depart until after the funeral on Monday. Diane Tepe supplied a huge tray of barbecued chicken to combine with the other meals of all varieties that kept arriving from our community of neighbors and friends. When there is nothing else that can be done, people respond with food. With additional cakes and cookies and fruit baskets that seemed to materialize on a minute-by-minute basis, there was more than enough to feed the welcome gathering of special people in our lives. With Irene once again joining forces with Diane to oversee the logistics of preparing all the food, our guests had no need of us but the comfort of their presence touched us beyond measure.

Our minds couldn't be completely cleared of the situation but there were many with us who singly could be the life of any party. Collectively, they represented a formidable force working against the powerful gloom that might have settled over us.

Still, the ever-present "if I can do anything" hung in the air on the rare occasions when the conversation lagged. I took Jerry Gares and Bud Caldwell aside at one point early in the afternoon and asked if they would mind going on an errand to Indian Mound Golf Course for us. Of course, they leaped at the chance to "do something" and happily escaped with their directive. I wanted to pay the owners of the course for the rounds that Gary had played during the week. When they returned and told me of the response of Sally and Paul Downing, owners of the club, my composure left me once again. They simply refused to take anything, saying that it was their privilege to get to know Gary.

Later, I mentioned casually that I might take a "dump run," a peculiarity reserved for those of us living in an extremely rural environment, especially in New Hampshire. Most of our visitors couldn't identify with a place that didn't have trash collection but my mention of going to the dump had the men in the group falling over themselves to make the trip one mile up the road. I protested that our dump foreman wouldn't recognize them. He likely would become a trifle testy if a group of men drove into the dump in a van with out-of-state plates. I really had to go, I told them, and they compromised by deciding that I could accompany them. It was, after all, a chance to "do something" tangible and it was not going to be wasted.

The trip was as eventful as one might have expected, hilarious even in its brevity. Fred Sargent, the foreman, is arguably the most well informed person on town matters since everyone must visit his facility and it serves well as an informal information center. When he saw Vince Riley's van full of people, his face registered a natural concern but his initial anxiety faded quickly when he saw me emerge from the van.

"They're all with me," I remember calling to him. His worried expression turned quickly to one of genuine compassion when he approached me. He shook my hand and told me how sorry he was to hear about Gary. Fred is known for his demanding operation of the dump; "runs a tight ship" is how most of the natives describe it. That day, as we tossed our trash bags over the edge of the landfill, his soft demeanor and understanding warmth touched all of us. I believe there were seven of us who went to the landfill that day, probably two for each of the trash bags we took with us. For most of them, their first simple excursion to a small town dump became an adventure and it was, after all, something that they could do.

The afternoon passed quickly and pleasantly, the camaraderie of the diverse group bridging the chasm between the sweet music of close friends and family and the discouragingly grim shadow of reality darkening the future. From my perspective, that afternoon presents a perfect argument against those who believe that it is possible to live in the present, leaving the future for God to man-age. Never have I wanted to live in the present more than that afternoon as each passing moment moved us closer to the evening visiting hours, a time that I would gladly have allowed God to manage for us. The harsh truth was that we were going to have to manage them; my anxiety level increased palpably as time inexorably crept on. The future may indeed rest in God's hands but He seems sometimes to have forgotten to instill in human nature the necessary trust required to accept that fact. This may be blasphemy but I will admit that I was depending much more on the human beings around me at the time to help me through the next twenty-four hours. In more rational times, I can think of them as God's agents but rationality was in short supply at the time. Subconsciously, I'm sure that I hoped that He would be close by but I, like our friends, was looking for something tangible. I wanted something as real as the several shrubs and plants given to us in Gary's honor and gracing our deck before planting.

*   *   *

"Someone once described a baby as a sweet new blossom of humanity, fresh fallen from God's own home to flower on earth," *our good friend Kathleen Whitehead wrote in the card accompanying a potted rhododendron bush. Early on Sunday morning, I had discovered her leaving the plant by our front door, not expecting to be caught. She refused to come in, not wanting to be "a bother." Her shrub was one of those waiting on the deck to be planted in Gary's Garden, a special area at the corner of our house. It is now the place that Nan has requested her ashes be scattered when she goes to join him.*

Kathleen's note continues.

"Plant this shrub, and each year as you admire its bright red flowers from your porch, be reminded of your sweet new blossom of humanity, who continued to blossom into such a fine young man. We hope you find strength in the many years of happy memories, knowing this world was a better place because of Gary's being here."

We planted the rhododendron, along with several other shrubs, rose bushes and flowers in Gary's Garden. It was too late for any blossoms that first spring but the bush flourished and we anticipated the promise of the flowers the next year.

In late October of that year, well after the first hard freeze of the season, we noticed that a bud had formed in the middle of the bush. Fascinated, I took photographs each day as it blossomed into a large, bright red flower.

"Highly unlikely," said the owner of the local nursery when I asked about the possibility of a single blossom occurring so deep into the fall. "But anything is possible in nature," he reminded me.

Another rogue blossom, I decided. I'm sure that is what it was---just another of those troublesome rogue blossoms.

*   *   *

"Paying my respects" or, worst yet, "paying my last respects" are the reasons most often given for attending the period known as calling or visiting hours. What an odd combination of words, even for a euphemism. All of us have probably used the expression at one time or another without realizing that it implies that we have a supply of "respects" that we are able to part with, like "paying my electric bill" implies that we have the dollars necessary to do it. Forgive this personal prejudice but it seems to me that a much more apt reason for running the gauntlet of visiting hours would be "saying my sorries" or even, "saying my last sorries," at least for this particular person. The night promised to be a long one, full of respects and sorries, and I felt terribly unprepared for it.

I've attended enough of these occasions to know how crushing they can be for the family of the deceased. Yet, they certainly serve a purpose. There is something positive that comes from the emotional strain and physical drain of greeting a continuous two-hour barrage of memory generators. I knew the line would include our friends, Gary's friends, family, former classmates, teachers, current and former professional colleagues, community acquaintances, long forgotten childhood friends and all the other categories of people who surely would come equipped with well meaning respects and sorries. What surprised me was that in some bizarre way, it was possible to dread an event while being excited about it at the same time. Perhaps my excitement came from the possibility that this evening might supply some of that mysterious element, the ephemeral closure that would keep me from railing against the utter injustice of it all.

*   *   *

All caskets are depressing but a special poignancy tempers the melancholia when one is enveloped with the American flag. What the symbolism of the flag draped casket lacks in subtlety, it makes up in power.

"This is a person," it screams, " a person who served his fellow man, unselfishly and for no personal gain."

Gary's flag adorned casket overpowered the large room where the visiting hours were to take place. The eight by ten photograph taken in his final year at West Point reflected the muted track lighting at the far end of the room as we entered. Flower arrangements created a multicolored backdrop that at times, I thought, clashed with the Stars and Stripes. We deliberately arrived well ahead of the scheduled beginning of the calling hours, partly to make certain that everything was in order but primarily to gather our strength in the unique environment of the funeral parlor. It is one thing to greet people at home, in familiar but emotional surroundings but another to be standing near our son's casket with the suffocating mixture of flower arrangements and antiseptic cleanliness permeating the air. We needed to adjust to that first before we could prepare for greeting the first of those about to come to "pay their last respects."

The evening went by with no surprises. Later, when the last of the visitors (They really can't be called guests, can they?) had gone, I realized how simple it would be to place everyone into categories. Unconsciously, we place the people who come and go in our lives into concentric circles. Our closest family inhabits the core circle, the haven that all of us rely upon in the most difficult times. The second circle consists of other family and close friends, people who are the second line of defense against the tribulations that are part of being human. Moving outward, each succeeding circle has less influence and impact on our lives. The theory is probably an oversimplification of the relationship of one human being to another but I've always felt that there is some truth to be found in it.

Many who came through the line during the two hours were people we had not seen at the wedding reception nor had we received them as visitors in our home after Gary died. Most of them resided somewhere in an outer circle but they had emotions to share and their respects (sorries) were heartfelt and genuine. Human emotions feed on each other and needs are met through the kind of personal contact that takes place during calling hours, no matter what the relationship is or was before. In spite of the difficulty of seeing people for the first time, we were grateful for their presence and for the strength gained by their emotional support.

Some people had to introduce themselves. The connection between us and them was the easiest to handle as it was generally a lower wattage emotional spark. A category that caused a substantial level of emotion were the old but now former friends whose lives had taken different turns from ours, close relationships that simply grew apart because life interfered. As one would expect, the depth of feeling when many of these people out of the past appeared varied with the role they had played in our lives.

Seeing a former colleague from the English Department at

Kingswood was the most difficult first time encounter I had the entire evening.

*   *   *

Ray Lord made me laugh. Teachers who do not maintain a solid and sometimes silly sense of humor often are in for long days in the classroom. When I came to Kingswood in 1970, Ray became my mentor. It was Ray who made department and staff meetings rock with his keen wit and occasionally outrageous sense of humor. It was Ray Lord who shared my tears of pride as he stood next to me at the annual Kingswood Academic Awards Assembly in the spring of 1980.

The Army colonel spoke for five full minutes about the value of a West Point education and the competitive nature of obtaining an appointment to the United State Military Academy. At the conclusion of his speech, he announced the appointment of Gary Scott Southard to the Class of 1984, United States Military Academy. The student body applauded loudly as Gary walked forward to accept the award and uncontrolled tears rolled down my cheeks. It was Ray Lord who put his arm around my shoulder and squeezed, whispering how fortunate I was to have a son like Gary.

Later in the assembly, Gary was presented with the Kingswood Good Citizenship Award, an honor that carried with it a two hundred and fifty-dollar cash prize. Ray shared that moment with me as well.

Within three days, Gary had used the money to buy a school-house clock that Barbara had wanted for the living room. The clock still hangs in our living room, close to the West Point sword he gave us for Christmas in his senior year.

* * *

Ray's appearance in the line filled me with apprehension. I knew that this was going to be quite a hurdle.

Now, here is another phenomenon that I find interesting. Some memories, when dragged to the surface, remain covered in the dust of time and an effort must be made to expose them. With others, the process of raising them seems to dissolve the dust away and when they reach the surface, they are crystal clear and ready to be relived. That's how the memories I just shared appeared when Ray reached me. Fortunately, there were only a few people in this category. I'm not at all sure that I would have had the strength to handle many more.

Many of Heidi and Gary's former classmates at Kingswood formed another major category. I had taught and coached some of them and was surprised that my reaction to them was not more emotional. In retrospect, I can try make myself believe that I needed to be strong so that their image of me didn't suffer but that doesn't ring true at all. I suppose that I think the real truth (Is there anything else but the "real" truth?) is that I had to be in shock at how adult they looked. They were young men and women who likely were attending a service for a dead classmate for the first time. They had moved out a few circles and time had separated them from me enough that they were actually strangers to me as adults. Their memories remained dust covered and that made me more melancholy than sad.

Another group of visitors might be classified as those who are in your life but not of it. They are the grocery store manager, the golf course owner and the insurance man, people whose kindness, compassion and sympathy allows them to acknowledge your pain by attending the calling hours. The emotional impact of their visit is muted and experienced at a more sublime level, making the connection easier to manage.

*   *   *

"We share each other's woes,
Each other's burdens bear;
And often for each other flows,
The sympathizing tear.
Blest Be The Tie That Binds
John Fawcett

The people of Melvin Village Community Church represented the only other sizable category and it was a group that would be a worthy test of our emotional stability. Church connections by their nature carry additional empathic baggage. In a small church such as Melvin Village, this is especially true. The sharing of worship services, fellowship activities, funerals, illnesses, prayers, fairs and auctions combine to draw people closer together, the "tie that binds our hearts in Christian love." These were people with whom we had shared many experiences and there was an enfolding haven with them should we need it. That evening, I recall that whenever one of these good people would move through the line, the expected struggle for control didn't materialize. It is yet another example of something that I can't explain but it was undeniable. I like to think that it was simply the "fellowship of kindred minds" at work.

Most other memories of that long evening come in disjointed bits and pieces. What I do know is that I felt the comfort of having so many of the people of the "inner circles" around. At difficult times, I had only to glance around the room and absorb the positive energies emanating from my relatives and friends.

The large room was set up in the way one would expect in that situation. The casket and flowers filled one of the narrow ends of the rectangle. We stood most of the evening but chairs were available for the family. Several rows of chairs faced the casket end of the room and in my mind I see those seats filled most of the time. A rather large open area spread out behind those seats and it is that area that projects a sharp memory whenever I permit it. I've decided that the same teacher quality that makes me tell someone in a theater audience to be quiet is at work with this memory.

The space became a gathering place for many of the visitors who had already passed through the line. What I have seen happen at "wakes" or calling hours or "viewings" is that some of the attendees lapse out of the gloom of the situation after passing through the "respects" part of the ritual. Sometimes, because the event brings together groups of people who may not have seen each other in a considerable time, the tendency to turn it into a reunion of sorts is a natural one. I'm sure that I've done the same. Funerals are wonderful places to catch up on news that otherwise would not be available.

My problem, and it was MY problem, not anyone else's, was that it was my son lying in the coffin not ten feet away from me. We were in one division of the room---the quiet section where any words that were spoken were in the proverbial hushed tones. The middle third of the room, the section with the chairs, served as a place for those who so desired might sit and pray or meditate or just watch as others proceeded through the line of family mourners. Those sitting in that section did converse quietly but not as softly as we did in the front.

It was the third section of the room that tested my patience during the entire evening. Perhaps it was the professional educator in me that forced a withering glare in that direction when a loud and boisterous conversation prevented me from hearing what a visitor was saying to me at my end of the room. The participants at that end of the room varied over the course of the night but the feeling I was experiencing was cumulative. The memory of that aspect of our night of paying respects is sharp and unrelenting. I wanted to scream; I wanted them to shut up; I wanted them to stop laughing; I guess I wanted them to stop being human. When I realized that, and I can only pray that my memory is correct on this, my anger and my impatience dried up, just so much wasted energy that was much better preserved for Monday, the day when we all hoped to feel the liberating sense of closure. I wasn't counting on it.

Chapter Nine
Monday, May 16, 1992
The Funeral

In an opening lesson plan of an Advance Composition course I taught at Kingswood, my notes say that I made the following observation while trying to convince the class that they all had the necessary tools to write.

"Everyone has experiences," I told them. "And all human beings have a need to relate those experiences. Even though what you've been through may not seem fresh and original, you are the world's leading authority on your own experience. Just remember that language is often subject to interpretation so clarity and specificity are essential."

The exhortation of my students is included here because this section of our story features my attempt to use language as a tool to bring back a day that I wish could be erased from my mind forever. I worry that my attempt will fail because that day is not delineated by visual images that may be scrolled across the tapestry of my mind and then shared. Instead, it is defined by a hopelessness and a desperate grasping for some sense of balance that seemed impossible to achieve.

The day of Gary's funeral promised to stop the descent, the day that the cliché of closure would reverse our trend and restart our lives once again. From the moment I awakened, the surrealism of the past several days paled when compared to what this day would bring. The service would begin at two o'clock in the afternoon, followed by a burial with full military honors at the Tuftonboro Townhouse Cemetery. Everyone was then invited to a reception at Willing Workers Hall, the church fellowship hall a short distance from the cemetery. Closure was just hours away or so it seemed.

The normal pattern for the passage of time continued through the morning. Time drags to a child anticipating the joys of Christmas but it accelerates to a frightening degree for the same child dreading his first filling by the dentist. An eagerly anticipated event arrives well beyond the time when we were prepared for it. The frightful one is sure to be upon us before we are ready.

The morning passed more quickly than I thought possible. Drop-in visits from many of the out-of-town guests occurred on a regular basis. For most, the extra day away from work created a considerable hardship and their brief visits that morning gave us the chance to thank them in an unhurried atmosphere, even though it could not be described as relaxed. By noon, the visits had stopped and we were left to do whatever one does to prepare for the next emotional onslaught.

We were instructed to arrive at the church by 1:30. As we entered the driveway, I was struck with the number of cars already filling the parking lot. We were to meet with Pastor Russ downstairs in the combination Sunday School/Fellowship Room, a small, inadequate space that was a prime motivator to succeed in a proposed expansion program. Since the addition project to the church remained out there on the time horizon somewhere, the family would be required to enter the church through the doors at the rear, proceeding down one of the two aisles.

The nature of the church building led many people to enter by way of the undercroft. The dramatic need for more space was never more evident as our quiet meditative time was continually interrupted by those attending the service. Approximately five minutes before the service was to begin, Russ Petrie said a prayer and led us up the stairs.

The first of many unmerciful slaps of reality struck me with the physical force of an unexpected shove while waiting in a movie theater line. I never expected to see the small church filled to overflowing. Extra rows of chairs had been set up in the chancel and even they were completely occupied. I knew without turning around that the balcony held its capacity. One clear memory of the moment when we started down the aisle of the church emerges from the shock of seeing so many people crammed into church.

I remember thinking how grateful I was that Pam's wedding had been at Perry Hollow. Had it been in the Melvin Village Community Church, I'm not sure if any of us could have made the walk down what would have been the same aisle. In addition to that, Gary's casket, the flag draped meticulously over it, was already in place, centered in the front of the church, exactly where the bride and groom would have been standing. I've heard it said that even in the most profound hopelessness, a small light of optimism will always exist. Had the wedding been held two days before in this church, the chance of any light existing in that setting lay somewhere between zero and nil.

The service that had been prepared had a deliberately bland feel to it. I've thought so often that I should have spoken at that service. I mean, who better than a father to eulogize his son? Now years removed from that day, I can say with absolute certainty that I would have performed a wonderful service to him had I done that. Unfortunately, this is another of those times that define so clearly the difference between a sweet imagination of what may have been and the depressing reality of what was. Simply put, my delivering a eulogy for Gary at that time was not even the briefest consideration. The courage to do so only comes when I know that there is no possibility for it ever to happen.

Describing the service as bland is somewhat unfair and needs further explanation. Bland has at least dozen synonyms, among them agreeable or pleasant. We all needed that; we needed something agreeable. The possibility for an intense, searingly emotional funeral surely existed but what this ninth day of the week from heaven and hell needed more than anything was "bland." After the initial shock of seeing the church so full, only two other moments from the service are powerful enough to emerge from the haze of the short funeral rite that day. One of them captures the essence of the image that so many had of Captain Gary Scott Southard, United States Army.

*   *   *

Understandably, Heidi didn't recall that Russ Petrie was with us when we went to her mother's house on the morning after Gary died. She did remember something that he said during his brief eulogy at the funeral.

"The one thing I remember about Pastor Petrie was something he said at Gary's service a few days later. It was something like 'I met Gary once at his family's home recently. My impression of him was a quick smile and a firm handshake.' I thought that such an accurate and keen observation of Gary."

It was an observation shared in almost the same words by several of my colleagues from Kennett who met him the day before he died.

*   *   *

At the conclusion of the service, Priscilla Gedney unintentionally provided another of the shocking slaps of reality. I was not aware that unless otherwise instructed, she would play "A Mighty Fortress Is Our God" as the closing hymn at funeral services. Since Barbara and I were married in a Lutheran church and I had adopted it as my religion, this traditional Lutheran hymn had become my favorite. In the hands of a skilled organist like Priscilla, the powerful music stirs the soul while bringing to mind the hopeful words of Martin Luther.

"Our helper he amid the flood, Of mortal ills prevailing. . ."

The crowded church, the resounding music, the two rows of family spiritually and symbolically if not physically clinging to each other, the casket a bare five feet way from us---where was that light of hope when we really needed it?

The plan for the addition to the church included an escape route for families attending funerals and an unobtrusive entrance for the male portion of wedding parties. The "new church" would have a side entrance that would allow the family to be escorted out as the remainder of the congregation waited to be guided out through the front. The logistics of our dismissal were different and, with the final hymn dissolving both Barbara and me, we were thankful that it happened the way it did. The family remained seated while the others were dismissed. The time was a blessing as it allowed us to regain our composure before venturing out to join the crowd gathered in front of the church waiting for the casket to be brought out.

*   *   *

The military color guard arrived in the morning from Fort Devens in Massachusetts. As one of the many military officers attending the funeral explained to me later, some army personnel receive specific training in what it means to provide a burial "with full military honors." The protocol is well defined, not surprising for any operation undertaken by the U.S. Army, and the contingent of eight soldiers knew their responsibilities well.

After we left the church, we joined the group assembled outside. I turned back toward the church quickly, my reddened eyes averting contact with any of the waiting group. I did notice my two library assistants from Kennett were in attendance and briefly wondered who had given them permission to close the library. After the draining moments of listening to "A Mighty Fortress. . ." the fresh air and beauty of the lake cleared my head somewhat. Everyone watched with curious interest as the burial with full military honors began to unfold before them.

The aisles in the church are narrow and the casket bearers had to lift their load to almost shoulder height to clear the pews on either side. As they approached the exit, I wondered how they would manage to maneuver the heavy load through the narrow doorway of the church. I recall how desperately I wanted everything to be over with. I suppose I was still grasping for that ever-illusive closure but at that point, the experience could only be described as grotesque. No closure was possible at that moment as the soldiers grappled with the awkward cargo.

My curiosity about the maneuvering through the doorway proved to be legitimate. The width of the casket barely allowed room for the pallbearers to squeeze through the doorway with it.

As they twisted and turned, my fear grew. For an interminably ghastly and sickening few seconds, I envisioned them dropping the casket and the contents spilling across the dooryard of the church. I sensed that the others waiting had sucked in their breath for the same reason. The worry soon was calmed as the first two reached the outside and stabilized their burden. The others held their military bearing as they exited and they then carried the casket solemnly down the walkway. After sliding the coffin into the hearse, the driver slammed the door closed, a little too cavalierly, I thought. I'm sure that I was being overly sensitive. Someone whose living depends upon the dead must find the realities of death easier to accept than the average person who encounters it infrequently so there was nothing personal in the slamming of the door. They have to be hardened somewhat, just as a man who pumps out septic systems for a living gets used to his job and its products. I obviously still had problems. That huge transition had not yet taken place in my heart. Even though his soul had long since departed, I still thought of the contents of that box as being our son and how dare he slam the door on him like that.

The soldiers left the church first and gathered at the cemetery to arrange the continuation of the military honors part of the program and to prepare to escort the mother and wife of their dead comrade to the gravesite.

*   *   *

For at least two weeks, I could not bring myself to use the word "dead" in connection with what happened to Gary. The memory of the first time I did is still with me. I remember it because I thought it was so noteworthy that I pointed it out to the gentlemen taking part in the conversation.

"That's the first time I've ever actually used the word dead when referring to him," I said to them. We had known each other only about one hour and were walking down the fourth fairway at Indian Mound. An innocent question about our children brought my first response, which I then must have felt obligated to follow with

an explanation. Later, when we became good friends with Ron Noble, one of the two, I asked him if he remembered me saying that. Well, guess what? He didn't. It is always surprising that we can become so self absorbed that we think that everything that is important to us assumes the same importance with others as well. Well, guess what? It doesn't.

*   *   *

The driver of the hearse waited until the family cars were arranged behind him then led the slow processional to the cemetery three miles away. Downtown Melvin Village doesn't have too many traffic jams in the middle of the afternoon but we had several local men who assisted in directing us out of the lot. I noticed not a single person observing our parade through the town.

The pallbearers were already at the hearse when we arrived at the cemetery. The whole process of extricating the casket and carrying it to the grave was flawless without the logistical challenges of the church. Barbara, her mother and Heidi were escorted to a small row of chairs that paralleled the grave, thoughtfully arranged facing northeast to avoid the blinding sun. The rest of us followed numbly along. Russ Petrie started the service as soon as he felt everyone was settled. Many of those who attended the graveside service stayed far in the background, some even lining the dirt road into the cemetery over fifty yards away and well out of hearing anything that was said. I remain puzzled by that but I think it may have been a gesture of respect for our privacy.

The poignancy of the traditional burial with full military honors lies in ritual. I had never attended such a burial and knew what to expect only from bits and pieces that I had seen in televised versions. The many West Point experiences we had with Pam and Gary had not softened my reaction to military ritual; what likely happened is that they enhanced the emotional impact of full dress parades and marching bands and bugle calls. It was about this time that what I've called in my own mind the "spectator syndrome" first appeared. Here we were, as intimately and as emotionally involved as it is possible to be, yet I felt as if I was watching a television news program. Is it possible to be attached and detached at the same time? I've decided that it is.

To my knowledge, we were not involved in the planning of the "Buried With Full Military Honors" scenario. I'm certain that Elliot Gruner, as a ranking officer and a West Point graduate, mentioned to us that he would handle that aspect of the process. What I know without equivocation is that the three rituals in this sort of ceremony confirmed my attachment/detachment theory.

I loved the seven-gun salute. What could be more impressive in our little town than the commands and then the firing of a salute? It occurred off in the distance, over by the townhouse. It seemed to come out of nowhere but nothing in the United States Army comes out of nowhere. It was the gun salute that caused my brother-in-law, standing directly behind me, to whisper, " Oh, Gary. . ." I wonder if he remembers uttering that simple two-word phrase. I should ask him but there are moments in time that are spoiled by close reexamination and I believe that may be one of those. So, I don't ask. It is simply there for me to relish when I need to. His anguish meant so much to me. Someday I'll have to tell him that. The echoing of those rifles across the field had to melt even the most cynical of anyone who heard them.

TAPS! I was thirteen when, in an unusually liberal mood, my father allowed me to accompany him to a showing of the film, *From Here To Eternity.* Robert E. Lee Pruitt plays taps for his murdered buddy and I believe that was the first time I learned the significance of that bugle call. I was a young boy, with my father and a few other adults, and I remember being embarrassed by the tears streaming down by cheeks. When the bugler sent the call of TAPS across the Tuftonboro Town Cemetery, I couldn't imagine any of those within hearing distance that didn't, at the very least, have tears in their eyes. I like to think that many, like me, searched frantically for a handkerchief to stem the swell of uninhibited emotion caused by that baleful wale of the bugle. I searched just as frantically for my belief, now hanging by the thinnest of threads, that all things happen for a purpose and this awful event MUST have a purpose.

Gary described the final part of that brief ceremony on numerous occasions. As a commanding officer, he memorized the required recitation. He was most impressed with the folding of the flag as the soldier contingent removed it from the casket. Some of them, he told me once, can remove it from the casket, fold it, and have it ready for presentation in less than two minutes.

Because there were two women receiving flags that day, one had been prefolded. That one was presented, with the required soliloquy, to Barbara. I stood behind her as she accepted the flag and listened as the junior officer, with a surprising amount of emotion in his voice considering that he didn't even know Gary, recited his speech.

The next few minutes caused me to smile, much as I smiled a few days before when the recalcitrant garage door balked after Gary had spent so much time on it. We all sat entranced as the "burial with full military honors" company worked on folding the flag for presentation to Heidi. I leaned over Barbara and whispered something to the effect that Gary would have been livid. After at least five minutes of folding and refolding the flag they had taken from Gary's casket, it was ready for presentation to his widow. (There is a word describing Heidi that was a long time entering my vocabulary.) Finally, the flag, folded properly, was presented to her and the required words were said. We were ready to move onto the next step in the ritual, a step that required none of the military personnel to be present. They assumed their formation and marched off toward their vehicles, literally into the sunset. Beautiful and vexatious are the words that I feel best describe that afternoon of ritual. Except for folding the flag and the minor juggling problem with the casket, the military honors were impressive but it was another of those instances where the beauty of what is happening clashes with the gloom of sadness settling over the scene.

The funeral director and assistants handed out roses to everyone. This is the final goodbye; the casting of the flowers on the casket of the loved one is yet another step toward that ultimate goal of finality.

* * *

One funeral in my memory included a step where the casket is actually lowered into the ground before the flowers are strewn over it. That was my mother's. We were given flowers and permitted to approach the casket AFTER it was lowered into the ground. Now, to me, that was serious closure.

* * *

Gary's casket remained above ground as we dropped our flowers and said our prayers. Not many people filed past the casket as it sat on the strapping waiting to be lowered. There is a limit to human endurance and most of us who were closely involved reached it that afternoon as we stared first at the hole then back to the casket. I for one wouldn't have been prepared for the closure of watching him lowered into the ground.

A few minutes later we returned to our cars and watched Heidi as she stood alone, staring at the casket. Our hearts were breaking for her. She had a single rose blossom in her hand and no one would dare to presume what thoughts occupied her mind. After several more minutes, Russ Petrie approached and put his arm around her shoulder. She seemed to accept the gesture graciously but I wondered if she might have considered that an intrusion. While preparing to write this section of the book, I thought of asking her what might have been in her mind during those moments. I did not; actually I could not. How could I or anyone presume to understand? Her thoughts during that time are as personal and private as any ever could be. Some things are better kept in the heart.

* * *

The Women's Guild of the Melvin Village Community Church responded in outstanding fashion, as they always have when asked to provide assistance in situations like these. The reception at

Willing Workers' Hall provided enough food for a large potluck supper. On any number of other occasions, I've returned to people's houses after a burial service for a reception and they have been gatherings that usually were light, overflowing with positive memories and revelations of personal anecdotes about the deceased. The somberness always seemed to disappear, as though the shared experiences of the past couple of hours coalesced into a single burden borne away by love. I anticipated the same transition when we returned to Willing Workers Hall for the reception but waiting there for us were a few more of those emotional hurdles that needed to be cleared first.

The arrangements at the church prevented us from seeing most of the people attending the funeral service in the church. The kindness and sympathy of so many additional people whom we had not yet seen touched us beyond words. There were people from the company of Bowers and Merena where Barbara worked. There were former colleagues of mine that I did not know were in attendance. Many people from the community showed their support by taking time out of the busyness of the day to come. There was a small contingent of fellow officers from Fort Carson, including Gary's commanding officer and major supporter, Lieutenant Colonel Joseph L. Yakovac.

*   *   *

"Truly outstanding. Smart, aggressive, caring and mission focused best describe this great soldier. CPT Southard is the best young leader I know. He outworks and outthinks contemporaries and the results show. His company is literally first in everything. I strongly recommend CPT Southard for early promotion. He will be a great battalion commander."

Joseph L. Yakovac, 6/14/91

"Unlimited potential. Will be a superb Battalion Executive Officer and should command a Bradley Battalion. Program for the most demanding and sensitive positions. Insure schooling and promotion well ahead of his contemporaries."

Jay L.Davis, Lieutenant Colonel
Battalion Commander
2/26/92

*　　*　　*

Barbara and I agreed afterward that the early part of the reception was as difficult as the calling hours. The congenial environment and wonderful food created an atmosphere that should have been more relaxed than the night before but the power of human emotion prevented that from happening. Just when one thinks there cannot possibly be any tears left, the good Lord supplies them in copious amounts. Just when one thinks that perhaps everything is not as bleak as it seems, it turns bleaker. As the humorous saying goes, "Cheer up, things could be worse. So I cheered up and, sure enough, things got worse."

However, it wasn't long before the positive power of all those around began to enfold us and the next phenomenon descended, filling us with a different kind of sadness.

The time was slipping away for many of those who had come so far and soon people began to say their good-byes. Looking at this from the advantage of the passage of time, I believe that the sadness of saying goodbye came from the subconscious realization that soon we would be alone to face the intimidating reality. The ready smile and the firm handshake, the good humor, the dedication, the "unlimited potential," the compassion and all the other traits that made our son the unique individual he was, were gone. As the last of the gathering left to disappear back into their own lives, the reception gradually came to an end and with a crushing, irrevocable finality, the nine-day week from heaven and hell ended as well.

Chapter Ten
A Cycle Completed
But
It Doesn't Get Any Easier

On Saturday, April 26, 2003, I attended the most entertaining and upbeat wedding ceremony of my life. Reverend Bill Brown, a Protestant minister, and Father Kevin Farmer, a Catholic priest, share the credit for the uniqueness of this service. They managed to blend a rollicking sense of humor with the poignancy and depth one expects from a solemn wedding ceremony. The cooperation and camaraderie between the two men created a memorable wedding but they made certain that the focus remained where it should be---on the bride and groom.

Pamela Southard Lohman and Dr. Robert Silcox, a veterinarian from Bel Air, Maryland are, by even the most objective standards, an exceptionally attractive couple. Even the two-dimensional photographs taken that day reveal the love they have for each other glistening in their eyes. I had never seen my self-assured daughter so nervous but when Pastor Bill Brown opened the ceremony with a hilarious joke, I sensed the ever-increasing tension of the preceding weeks begin to subside. Every aspect of the well planned ceremony fell into place, the humorous by-play between the Pastor Bill and Father Kevin continuing unabated and relieving any residual anxiety with each passing moment. When the marital rites were completed, the traditional receiving line formed, followed by the obligatory pictures of endless combinations of wedding party and family.

With the rituals and customs over, the White family, Barbara and I climbed into the van for the ride to the reception at the Top Of The Bay Officers' Club at Aberdeen Proving Grounds, forty minutes from the church. Almost eleven years had passed since Gary had died two days before Pam's first marriage. Until that ride between the wedding and the reception, I was not aware that our entire family had been talking to him the whole week, each with different yet related agendas. All of the conversations assumed various forms of requests for help.

* * *

The weather forecast for Pam and Bob's wedding sounded ominous and hopeless. The heavy rain that inundated the Baltimore area on the morning of April 26, 2003 was expected to continue throughout the day with just a slim chance of even a brief respite. I, as the father of the bride, could only fume, raging silently at the unfairness of it all. This one should be perfect, I remember thinking as I stared out at the deluge. The tradition that rain on a wedding day is a sign of good luck may have some merit. However, I have the feeling it originated long ago to erase the tears of a bride who saw her special day ruined by a drenching rain similar to what was happening in Cockeysville, Maryland that day.

* * *

On more occasions than I could count, a harmless memory broached at a family gathering has unleashed the emotional freight train that would then careen down the tracks, often out of control. I believe that is why members of our family did not mention any of their one-sided conversations with our late son in the time leading up to Pam's wedding, as if bringing up the fears of dreaded associations with her first marriage would affect this one.

As we drove to the reception, with the wedding over and without any glitches, Jeri ventured out onto the thin ice that covered the pond of memories of Gary. Barbara quickly joined in and soon we all knew that Gary was a powerful, almost physical presence in our hearts and minds as Pam's wedding approached.

* * *

The photographer arrived shortly after noon, even though the wedding was hours away. She planned the traditional indoor preparation photographs, the dressing, the hairdos, the facials and the camaraderie of the women in the wedding party, noting that the idea of taking any of the planned outdoor photos would be out of the question due to the horrific weather. I was impressed with her professionalism and flexibility, her demeanor and helpfulness actually relieving some of the depression over the outside gloominess that threatened to dampen the boisterous spirits of Pam and her attendants and friends.

*   *   *

Barbara and Jeri agreed that they awoke in the morning telling Gary that he really MUST do something about the weather. As the conversation continued, we learned that during the days before, both had been asking that Gary "use his influence" to make sure that this wedding be a happy occasion, memorable for its own sake. On the morning of the wedding, they decided to be much more specific.

*   *   *

The first coincidence but not the most telling was the cessation of the rain. As the morning turned into afternoon, the forecast had not improved. No one was being greedy. Sunshine was not required; all we asked was for the rain to let up a bit so dresses were not ruined; shoes were not squishy; hair was not hanging in dripping ringlets.

The time schedule proceeded and the "girls" were dressed in time for the outdoor pictures without any hope that there would be any. The "boys" were all dressed in their tuxedos and ready as well. It really doesn't matter who made the first observation but it sent people scurrying to the window. The rain had stopped. After a brief ten-minute wait, the photographer announced that she was ready to chance her expensive equipment to the elements and all ventured hesitantly outside. Despite the heavy cloud cover that afternoon, the first pages of the wedding album are filled with beautiful pictures of the wedding party taken outside Pam's house on a day that had been declared a washout by virtually every weather-man in the area. Not another drop of rain fell during the afternoon.

* * *

Lacking some quite unusual circumstance, the bride and groom constitute the focus of attention in a wedding ceremony. Reverend Brown and Father Farmer made certain that this was the case. However, the conversation on the way to the reception shifted to a phenomenon that Jeri and I had noticed at some point during the service. Barbara, intent and engaged in the wedding ceremony, admitted that she had missed it while Duane, Ryan and Dex were aware of it as well.

* * *

Our friend, Gary Tepe, was the first at the reception to mention it. He remembered it happening toward the end of the ceremony, around the time of the exchanging of vows. Others at the reception mentioned it as well.

"Just a little coincidence," I'm sure I replied. At least, I'm sure I said something like that in response.

It really wasn't that big a deal. Or was it? In the spring of the year in Maryland, I'm sure there are days that are "washouts" yet have a peak of sun at some point during the day.

"Amazing!"

"Beautiful"

Those words, among others, were used to describe the sun choosing that exact time to briefly appear between the heavy clouds to shine through the stained glass window, splashing its light across the sanctuary of the church and over the wedding party. I wish I could say it rested on the faces of the bride and groom but I'm not sure that would be accurate.

What I can say is that it was "a wonderful coincidence" and leave it at that, although anyone who knows me is aware of how I feel about coincidences now.

There are none!

*   *   *

"Does it get any easier?" I've been asked this question more times than I could count. Over the years, my answer has been the same as it was after one year and I'm now certain that it will be the same right into eternity.

"Of course it doesn't get any easier," I'll say, as gently as I can. "It just hurts a little less." We lost a son and the world lost a fine human being but it is not like this is anything new. I've known people who have suffered tragedy far beyond what our family did yet they continue to function admirably. I believe they move forward only because it hurts a little less, not because it gets any easier. Many examples could be used to illustrate the subtle difference between the two. Sharing just a few might be helpful.

*   *   *

The room where Gary stayed was just as he left it when he drove his grandmother to her doctor's appointment. We had gone in to find his Harry Connick suit but had not disturbed anything else. The room is at the end of the upstairs hall and it is practically impossible to avoid looking into it for anyone in that hall. Until after the funeral on Monday, we had kept the door closed. The memories abiding in that room, the same one he occupied for ten years before going to West Point, could have assumed a life of their own. In the first day or two after he died, I believe we could have sealed that room and its memories without hesitation.

My first real excursion in to the room was after we returned from the funeral. I could not do it the first day but four days later, it wasn't any easier but it did hurt less.

*   *   *

In the late spring of 1992, Kennett High School held its annual assembly for inducting new members into the National Honor Society. I've always enjoyed these events in any high school as they recognize those students who excel academically, allowing for a temporary commandeering of the pedestals usually reserved for the athletes in a school. I looked forward to attending the assembly and was happy to be asked again to host the reception for the students, parents and teachers in the Kennett Library. Gary had died less than three weeks before. Gatherings of this sort are truly uplifting; the youthful vitality and enthusiasm is palpable and pride lights the faces of the parents. What I did not anticipate was the effect the assembly would have on me.

Early in the program, a well-dressed young man, a senior, lit the candle of truth or honesty; I'm not sure which. Before he began to speak, that simple motion acted as a time machine to the past and I could see Gary years before, doing exactly the same thing. Fortunately, my duties as a librarian did not require sitting among the students with a class so I was standing relatively close to the exit. The entire student body was in the assembly and the halls, again luckily, were completely empty as I walked briskly to the library, tears stinging my eyes. I did not want to see anyone. After leaving a note to my capable assistants asking them to assume the hosting responsibilities, I left the building as quickly as I could. The twenty-mile drive down Route 16 that day was a blur.

The parking lot at Indian Mound Golf Club was virtually empty. For reasons I can't explain, I stopped there, went to the club storage for my clubs and, with no one on the first tee, stepped up and teed off. I played the nine holes alone, dressed in my school clothes, in every bit as emotional a state as I had been anytime since Gary had died. In retrospect, the behavior was rather bizarre but at the time it felt like the right thing to do. I never gave it a second thought.

A long hill separates the last green from the clubhouse and by the end of the climb, I felt somewhat in control again. After putting my clubs back in storage and walking past the pro shop, Paul

Downey called to me through the window. He has a keen sense of humor and hollered something like "Are you going for the best dressed golfer award?" It was then I realized that my tie was still tightly pulled up to my neck!

The passage of three weeks had not made it any easier but perhaps that nine holes of golf, played with a strong but unidentifiable presence and serving a minor cathartic purpose, somehow made it hurt just a tiny bit less.

*   *   *

The reality waves hit when least expected and their triggers are often a mystery. They can strike with a physical force that can buckle the knees and shorten the breath.

Three months after Gary's death, we traveled to Colorado Springs to visit with Heidi. Pam coordinated some leave time and met us there. We arrived at the beautiful house in mid-afternoon, the dazzling view of Pike's Peak highlighted by the bright Colorado sun. Heidi was not due home from work for several hours and we unpacked and settled in after the long trip. I was walking around the second floor and had gone into the computer room that Gary had described to me in great detail. The unexpected wave struck shortly after I entered that room. I remember feeling an overwhelming sadness and easing out of the room backward. I was shaking when I reached the bedroom where we were staying. I sat on the bed before my knees gave way.

First nostalgia than sadness brought on by the memories gives the crashing waves of reality their power.

Clothing . . . "personal effects" . . . memorabilia . . . I avoided what I knew would be a most powerful wave but Barbara and Heidi did not. Several days into our visit, Heidi suggested we look through Gary's clothes and some other items that she thought we might want to keep. I was doing some minor painting around the house and used that as my lame excuse to keep from dealing with the difficult issues that arise from such a simple task as sorting through a pile of clothing and a few knick-knacks.

Several hours later that task was finished and I could tell without even asking how strong the wave had been for both of them. I think it is one thing to carry armloads of clothing to a storage area but quite another to sift through individual pieces. The armload is not specific but each T-shirt or sweat suit or sport coat or key chain is capable of triggering a happy memory that instantly turns sad. I'm glad I had painting to do that day.

Whether it was the National Honor Society ceremony or the home that breathed the life of Gary three months later, it wasn't getting any easier but each day of our visit, it hurt just a little bit less.

*   *   *

The member-guest golf tournament at Indian Mound was a favorite event of mine. As a member, I was able to invite a guest for what would be a weekend of golf and camaraderie and who knows, perhaps even victory! In the fourth summer after Gary's death, my guest would be Jeri's husband, Duane. There was no cause for me to be expecting a wave on this occasion. The excitement of participating in a golf tournament can be all-consuming. That Saturday morning, I planned on meeting Duane at the course early for some practice and strategy sessions. (As if that would help us!)

My mind was on the competition that morning as I set out for the course. Duane would be a great partner and I was anticipating a good day of golf and "bonding" with my son-in-law. Indian Mound is about ten miles to the north of our house, across Durgin Road through rural, sparsely populated countryside. It is the route I traveled for ten years to Kennett and I've crossed it hundreds if not thousands of times. Nothing eventful ever happens on this street and I certainly didn't anticipate one of those reality whitecaps breaking over me on that particular morning.

This wave fell into the "will never happen" category of sadness. The thought first came as I reviewed other partners I might have for this tournament in the future and Gary's face appeared. Then, the crushing reality settled over me. That is never going to happen.

NEVER! Here it was, four years later and yet the tears cascaded down my cheeks. I found a place to pull over and tried to regain my composure. I must have sat there for ten minutes and I don't remember a single car passing by. Finally, I was ready to go somewhere. I looked in both directions, preparing to make a U-turn and go home. Then, a simple awareness swept through me. I was looking in the rear view mirror in more ways than one. I couldn't go home. I put the car in gear and started down the road toward the golf course. It wasn't any easier; it just didn't hurt as much.

*   *   *

Now, years later, the frequency of the waves has diminished. Like the unexpected breaker can send a bather tumbling headfirst into the surf, these may do the same. But, because we have experienced so many of them and are more prepared for the breathtaking power they have, we can minimize their damage. They are not any easier to handle than they were ten years ago but their reality is just a bit less painful.

With the support and love of our family, our friends, our faith, our community and our church, we have been able to move on and we are thankful for that. Time has not made anything easier. The loss of such a worthwhile person in a world that cries out for compassionate people remains a question that I hope and pray I'll have answered some day. Until then, the memories will have to suffice as they will have to suffice for the special people mentioned in this book who have now passed on as well. In some unique, inexplicable way, I enjoy a comfortable feeling knowing that there is quite a contingent of people I have known who now know the answer to that mystifying question---Why?

*   *   *

Gary sent this poem to the wife of his West Point sponsoring officer when she was very ill in 1982. He was only twenty years old at the time.

"What you may not know is how hard Gary worked when I was ill to help me through that time," Nancy Wise wrote in her sympathy card. I believe it epitomizes the kind of person he had become, even at the tender age of not quite twenty-one.

The Weaver

My life is but a weaving
Between my Lord and me.
I cannot choose the colors
He worketh steadily.

Oftimes he weaveth sorrow
And I in foolish pride
Forget He sees the upper
And I the under-side.

Not til the loom is silent
And shuttles cease to fly,
Shall God unroll the canvas
And explain the reason"Why?"

The dark threads are as needful
In the Weaver's skillful hand
As the threads of gold and silver
In the pattern life has planned.

Author unknown

Think about THAT!

LaVergne, TN USA
04 January 2010

168688LV00005BA/2/P

9 781604 943825